RECLAIMING THE AUTHENTIC SELF

Dynamic Psychotherapy with Gay Men

Carlton Cornett, LCSW

JASON ARONSON INC.
Northvale, New Jersey
London

This book was set in 11 point Bookman by TechType of Upper Saddle River, New Jersey, and printed and bound by Haddon Craftsmen of Scranton, Pennsylvania.

Library of Congress Cataloging-in-Publication Data

Cornett, Carlton.
    Reclaiming the authentic self : dynamic psychotherapy with gay men
    / by Carlton Cornett.
        p. cm.
    Includes bibliographical references (p.   ) and index.
    ISBN 1-56821-395-6
    1. Gay men—Mental health.   2. Psychodynamic psychotherapy.
    3. Psychotherapist and patient.   I. Title.
    RC451.4.G39C67   1995
    616.89′14′086642—dc20   94-24827

Manufactured in the United States of America. Jason Aronson Inc. offers books and cassettes. For information and catalog write to Jason Aronson Inc., 230 Livingston Street, Northvale, New Jersey 07647.

For DeWayne

A man who champions the cause of gay men and lesbians. A man who cares deeply about justice for everyone who is oppressed. A man who teaches me daily about love, kindness, tolerance, and compassion. I am grateful that he is my lover and the meaning of my life.

Contents

Preface

This is a book about creating an environment that invites patients to discover and create their authentic identities and sustains them as they do so. I will describe some specific circumstances, primarily involving the internalization of negative societal values toward homosexuality, that produce difficulties for many gay men. This internalization of an anti-homosexual bias—which arises and is maintained through social interaction—necessitates an understanding of psychotherapy as an enterprise in which the relationship between the two participants is the preeminent feature.

This is not a text on technique in the traditional sense of that term. I believe that technique as it is often described, rather than being the primary element of psychotherapy, is of secondary importance. It is the relationship between the two participants in the psychotherapeutic experience that can be growth-producing, creative, and valuable to the patient. If this relationship is characterized by qualities that affirm and sustain them, patients generally experience the encounter with the psychotherapist as helpful and valuable. If the relationship is not characterized by these qualities, no technical intervention can offer a similarly helpful or valued experience. This is especially true with gay men. The technique I will present is primarily composed of the perspective and skills involved in creating an authentic and responsive relationship between two people.

This is a book about gay men because that is where my primary expertise lies. The principles outlined on the pages that follow are, I think, applicable to psychotherapy with lesbians and many other groups of patients. However, as my experience is primarily in working with gay men, I actively avoid generalizations to other groups. I leave it to others who have more expertise in working with other groups of patients to extend or modify the principles proposed.

As a means of providing an explanation for my perspective, I often make generalizations regarding gay men, their dynamics, and their development. Generalizations tend to dismiss the uniqueness of each individual and are therefore suspect any time they are introduced into discussions of psychotherapy. Beyond that, however, generalizations introduced into discussions of psychotherapeutic practice have often led to pathologization. Especially in a time when forces of the political and religious right are renewing efforts to pathologize (and in some cases, demonize) homosexuality, it is important to state that a discussion of the differential dynamics between homosexual and heterosexual men does not mean that either is inherently inferior. If we lived in a predominantly homosexual culture, one could expect to see discussions of heterosexual men attempting to adapt and thrive in that culture. But, we do not live in such a culture, and so this book is about homosexual men attempting to live and thrive in a heterosexual culture and ways that a psychotherapist may be of assistance to them in this regard.

This book is about psychotherapy that respects and integrates the traditions of psychoanalytic theory and dynamic existentialism. Therefore, I discuss topics typically seen in the psychoanalytic literature and attempt to adapt these to a perspective more amenable to the difficulties of gay men. The result is decidedly existential. This book also finds me revealing much about myself, which is a rarity in the traditional psychodynamic literature. It has been in the small, although, thankfully, growing number of psychodynamic works that allow a glimpse of the author's authenticity and fragile humanity, that I have found the most memorable lessons. For that reason I have not attempted to disguise myself in these pages as "one psychotherapist" or "a clinician." It is my hope that this adds to the readability of the pages that follow, as well as the message they attempt to impart.

Carlton Cornett, LCSW
Nashville, Tennessee

Acknowledgments

It is a great pleasure to express my sincere appreciation to the following people.

First, my lover, DeWayne Fulton. He has read and reread drafts of this book without complaint. He has lent his formidable writing and editing skills to ensure that it did not become a compendium of psychobabble. Much more than this, though, he continually offers me a relationship that is nurturing, supportive, and loving. His encouragement and support are the basis for every project in my life.

Second, Ross A. Hudson, LCSW, whom I have been privileged to call my best friend throughout my adult life. Throughout my career he has offered support, intellectual stimulation, and a belief that I have something to say that may interest other professionals. He, too, has read through each draft of the book and offered invaluable suggestions regarding both content and style.

For his assistance in helping me understand the value of my own authenticity, I wish to thank Volney P. Gay, Ph.D.

I also wish to thank the staff of the Vanderbilt Independence Development Center, who, in addition to being a superb group of people to work with, have been patient with me while I have been writing this book.

I also appreciate the interest that Jason Aronson has shown in my work. His staff: Michael Moskowitz, Judy Cohen, Nancy D'Arrigo, and especially Norma Pomerantz who has always listened patiently and supportively to my many questions through two books, have been professional and helpful.

I wish to express my appreciation to our "children": Christopher, Michael, Trajan, Forster, Theo, Rajah, Salem, Sox, and Jasmine, who missed many opportunities for brushing, wrestling, and snuggling while I sat in front of the computer screen.

Finally, to my patients I extend my deepest appreciation for the many lessons I have learned from them that have enriched my life.

I

THEORETICAL ISSUES

1

The Centrality of Identity

Existence may have no objective meaning, but it does not mean nothing, otherwise meaning would mean nothing.

R. D. Laing

For real psychotherapy is not concerned primarily with adaptation to any kind of reality, but with the adjustment of the patient to himself, that is, with his acceptance of his own individuality or of that part of his personality which he has formerly denied.

Otto Rank

A PERSONAL JOURNEY

Over the past ten years I have had the opportunity to work with hundreds of gay men. They have sought treatment for a variety of reasons, including problems involving relationships, job satisfaction, sexual dysfunction, anxiety, depression, anger, and adjustment to changes brought about by the Acquired Immunodeficiency Syndrome (AIDS). Initially, I attempted to understand these problems from a fairly traditional psychoanalytic framework. I had become interested in psychoanalytic theory as a graduate student. It seemed rich in potential to explain many human phenomena that seemed confusing and contradictory to an outside observer. Psychodynamic theory offered a view of the person as rich and complex; it attempted to capture the sense of mystery and elegance of life, which the reductionistic behavioral, cognitive, and biological paradigms coming into vogue seemed so eager to dismiss.

After graduation, as I listened to my patients describe the most intimate aspects of their lives, I was poised to hear evidence of drive derivatives and ego defenses. I was concerned with maintaining an appropriate frame (Langs 1976, 1982) and analytic attitude (Schafer 1983). My understanding of *technique* centered on short, precise interpretations. Each word of an interpretation was carefully chosen to avoid moving too quickly (while moving quickly enough), uncovering too deeply (while uncovering deeply enough), but yet maintaining neutrality and anonymity, while also remaining empathic. A complex, if not impossible, task.

I discovered over an agonizing period of time (agonizing for both my patients and me) that this approach was simply not helping me understand the distress that these men brought to my office. My approach was not enabling them to understand the basis of their distress any more fully, nor was it facilitating any change in their life circumstances, and at that time, change was my concept of the ultimate psychotherapeutic goal. I experienced myself more and more as a clinician emotionally present for my patients solely or primarily because of my emotional absence (Laing 1969).

This set of circumstances did, however, initiate a desire for change in me. At times I desired a change of career; at other times my goal was more modest and involved simply finding a model of psychotherapy that offered more freedom and room for human connection. However, time and again I would return to a fundamental belief that psychoanalytic theory offers the best of what we know to our patients.

My seemingly intractable ambivalence was not aided by my first experience with my own psychoanalytic treatment. My first therapist was a fairly traditional analyst who said little. When he did speak it was in terse interpretations that often had a pejorative feel to them. He saw my "overwhelming need for control," my "schizoid adaptation," my homosexuality, and an incomplete resolution of the oedipal conflict as the basic difficulties in my life. He was consistently anonymous, generally neutral in the traditional sense of this term (with deviations in neutrality falling somewhere along the continuum of chastisement), and invariably interpretive. He also practiced therapeutic abstinence as I then understood it. I certainly got no idea that he cared about me, although there was the periodic sense that he found me somehow distasteful. I left this treatment feeling that I had experienced *real* psychoanalytic psychotherapy and I was all the more dejected for it.

These experiences with my patients and my own

therapy were partially the result of my inexperience and psychopathology. However, to conclude that these factors were the sole foundation upon which these experiences were constructed is an oversimplification. Such a conclusion also flies in the face of a growing literature by analysts and analytically oriented psychotherapists that describes their first contacts with analytic treatment as disappointing at best and traumatic at worst (Little 1990, Masson 1990, Menaker 1989). However, in these cases, as was true for me as well, these clinicians' early disappointing experiences did not result in a complete rejection of psychoanalytic theory, but in a search for ways to translate it into a relevant system for understanding their own dynamics and those of their patients.

I originally believed that all psychological phenomena could be explained through traditional ego psychological theory. Further, I believed that all adult experiences, including those of gay men, could be understood in the context of oedipal and psychosocial development (Erikson 1963). Given this belief, a technique focused on resolving oedipal difficulties followed naturally. However, all this changed through three distinct events in my life. The first was my own psychotherapy, which helped me understand little about myself and was so narcissistically injurious in the process. The second was the discovery of the work of Heinz Kohut (1977, 1984) and a second analytic treatment with a self psychologically oriented psychoanalyst. The final event that changed my thinking about psychotherapy, especially with gay men, was my first contact with a gay man who was struggling with AIDS. This experience led me to dynamic existential theory and has resulted in my attempts to integrate self psychology and dynamic existential theory.

As a gay man I have always had a particular interest in the development of gay men and the difficulties that bring them to consult a psychotherapist. While I have never consciously believed that homosexuality is pathological in itself, my early attempts at working with gay men sprang from a conception of human development that offered little support to any outcome not representing an adequate (i.e., heterosexual) oedipal resolution. I employed a technical stance that originated to elicit a transferential re-creation of oedipal dynamics, which could then be resolved interpretively. This stance, free-floating attention notwithstanding, offered a focus for listening to patients and a way of organizing what was heard. The problem, which took some time and a great deal of soul-searching and study to grasp, was that I did not and do not believe that inadequate oedipal resolution is the basis for most of the difficulties that bring gay men to psychotherapy.

Kohut (1977, 1984) started my search for the possibility that there might be another legitimate focus of clinical work. His emphasis on the development of the capacity to maintain self-esteem and a coherent internal image of the self (i.e., the experience of "I") seemed particularly important in thinking about gay men, who face almost daily challenges to their esteem and identity. In Kohut's hands narcissism became a word with explanatory power, rather than a way to clinically devalue patients. Especially in his later writings, Kohut diminished the importance of the oedipal conflict in understanding developmental and clinical phenomena. This has been one of the most controversial aspects of self psychology.

Isay (1989) has examined oedipal development in homosexual men and from this examination has offered the revolutionary proposal that it follows a different path than does oedipal development for heterosexual men. This idea revitalizes a conception of development that includes an oedipal phase. It also encourages those of us who work with gay men to avoid pitching the baby out with the bathwater.

From my own work, though, it is seldom oedipal material that forms the basis for a therapeutic encounter that the patient regards as successful. Primarily, it seems to be the most basic work of responding as an empathic selfobject that leads to the patient developing a sense of his own unique and valuable self. This is the central tenet of both Kohut's model and that of the existential school. It is a stance that is particularly helpful in working with gay men.

IDENTITY AND MEANING

The introduction of self-esteem and identity cohesion as foci of psychotherapy opens a door to understanding *meaning* in life. This became clear to me as I worked with my first gay male patient who was living with AIDS. This experience taught me much about the inseparability of the development of personal identity from meaning in life.

We began psychotherapy in 1985 as the AIDS epidemic was first asserting itself in southern cities. Most of us knew very little about this syndrome (a situation I fear has changed very little despite protes tations to the contrary by the scientific and medical communities). There were conflicting theories about its genesis and whether or not it was caused by the Human Immunodeficiency Virus (HIV). We did not then, and do not now, know if one who tested positive for antibodies to this virus would invariably go on to develop full-blown AIDS (Jennings 1993, Root-Bernstein 1993, Thomas et al. 1994). Those who tested positive for antibodies to the virus then, and to some extent still, often had the feeling of being part of a cosmic crapshoot. If they were lucky, they would not develop AIDS; if not, then they would. There seemed to be no rhyme or reason as to who did and who did not develop the full-blown syndrome. Over the years I have come to discover that most gay men fully expect to develop AIDS after HIV infection no matter what they say consciously to reassure themselves and those around them. My patient was no exception.

When he first came to my office he had just been released from a psychiatric unit in a large metropolitan hospital. He had been hospitalized after a suicide attempt that very nearly achieved its ostensible goal. The hospital staff diagnosed him as being depressed. He was placed on an antidepressant and he improved. However, during his hospitalization he also discovered that he was HIV positive. This seems to have been addressed at the hospital ambivalently through stern admonitions to engage in safe sex with uninfected men (at that time some physicians were unconcerned about the consequences of two HIV-infected men having unprotected sex because the idea of differential strains of the virus and reinfection had not become popularly known) and to avoid excessive worry because there was a good chance that he would never go on to develop AIDS.

He came to the clinic at which I worked because it accepted patients on a sliding-fee schedule. He had seasonal employment as a construction laborer (and was currently out of work) and had no insurance. Like most agencies that work on a sliding-fee basis, this one had a number of students and young practitioners. I fell primarily into the latter category but this man was to expand my perpective on psychotherapy a great deal and I was fortunate indeed to have been his student.

The details of his treatment are of less importance to this discussion than what I began to learn about effective psychotherapy as I listened to him tell me his life story over a year's time. As he talked about his history, his successes and failures, his hopes and fears, it became increasingly clear that while traditional ego psychology could be of great help in understanding him, it was incomplete. What this patient struggled with at that point in his life was a search for meaning. He described himself as feeling empty, and said that he did not know who he was. More than anything else, this led to the "depression" that resulted in the suicide attempt (although I grew to understand with him that this act was not truly an attempt to end his life, because he had no clear sense of an identity he wished to destroy). Certainly he was trying to adapt to changing circumstances in his life. He was also certainly influenced in his attempts at adaptation by his developmental history. However, to see the struggle that brought him to psychotherapy in those terms alone, as traditional psychoanalytic theory encourages, would be to miss completely the most central element of his life: he desperately sought to develop a coherent identity that filled the emptiness he experienced. He was alienated from the core values, feelings, and memories that made up who he genuinely was and provided meaning, coherence, and purpose in his life.This early case was instrumental in challenging me to expand my view of psychoanalytic theory to include more than ego psychology.

Ego psychology, beginning with Anna Freud (1966) and Hartmann (1939), challenged psychoanalytic theory to see the human being as more than a collection of drives pressing for release with varying intensity. It suggested that people are complex creatures who maintain commerce with the external world and in so doing make use of an array of adaptive systems whose goal is to ensure as closely as possible that the individual's internal world corresponds to the external. These systems then give the person a sense of continuity and congruence that allows for object relatedness and more complete drive satisfaction.

The emphasis placed upon the adaptive capacities of the ego added dramatically to the explanatory power of psychoanalysis. However, while ego psychology greatly expanded the psychoanalytic view of the complexity of the person, it also fell into the same philosophical trap as id psychology in that it reduced human life to a set of capacities, with little room for understanding the person as an agent of action, searching ultimately for meaning in life, rather than as a collection of reactions dictated by early development. My year working with the patient described earlier began to move me away from viewing people generally, but gay men especially, as primarily motivated by adaptation to viewing them as motivated by a desire to understand themselves and their lives in all their complex and authentic varieties.

When one works with anyone facing a life-threatening illness or who is recovering from the loss of someone who was dearly loved, the importance of meaning in life manifests itself very dramatically. When I began my practice, AIDS was very much a confusing and frustrating daily reality for most gay men. Almost all of us knew someone—a friend, a lover, a neighbor—who was struggling with it. The specter of AIDS haunted us almost every day in one form or another. It still does in myriad subtle ways. AIDS has brought little of any real value to the world; however, it has provided a context in which the centrality of the search for personal meaning in psychotherapy can be seen most clearly.

In the chapters that follow I will describe an approach to psychotherapy with gay men that offers them a relationship through which they can become deeply acquainted with themselves. This approach invites an exploration of that which is authentic in the self. It is an approach that emphasizes identity— and thus, meaning. It attempts to give clinical form in work with gay men to Laing's (1967) definition of psychotherapy as the *"obstinate attempt of two people to recover the wholeness of being human through the relationship between them"* (p. 53, italics in the original).

Although this approach is influenced not only by self psychology and existential dynamic theory but also by psychosocial, object relations, and interpersonal theory, my description of it makes liberal use of the language of self psychology. Self psychology, of all psychodynamic theories, has come closest to capturing the nuances of the human encounter between two people engaged in psychotherapy. It also avoids the sometimes esoteric and clinically impractical language of existential theory. However, I also believe that self psychology is at its foundation an existential dynamic theory (Cornett 1992a,b, Gottesfeld 1984).

In addition to providing a language that has more currency and accessibility to a larger group of psychodynamic clinicians, self psychology also offers a conceptual advantage when integrated with existential theory over either theory alone. This advantage lies in its articulation of a developmental theory that accounts for identity emergence and maturation. Existential clinical theorists tend to focus on the *assertion* of identity, including the capacity to achieve an acknowledgment and acceptance of one's ultimate aloneness in the world; the capacity to accept responsibility for one's life and all its emotional, psychological, and behavioral consequences; the capacity to accept one's ultimate freedom; and the capacity to accept and assert one's will in interaction with oneself and the external world (Fromm 1969, May 1953, Rank 1964, Sartre 1957). Although these theorists acknowledge the paramount role played by identity in the development and maturation of these capacities (e.g. May 1953), they have not articulated a cogent developmental model that focuses on identity. Yalom (1980) is a notable exception, although his model of development stresses the differentiation of identity in juxtaposition to the awareness and acceptance of the inevitability of death. Self psychology offers a model that provides an explanation for the varying levels of maturity achieved in the assertion of one's identity because it offers an explanation of differing levels of maturity (e.g., cohesion, integration) of the self.

A NOTE ABOUT TECHNIQUE

This is not a book on technique in the sense in which most dynamic psychotherapists think of it. There is no description of the correct manner of offering interpretations, confronting, and so on. What the psychotherapist says to a patient is important; however, it is important primarily as it relates, positively or negatively, to the type of relational environment that the therapist and patient create together. No activity of the therapist can be separated from this environment. I have, as a result, chosen to focus extensively on the relational qualities of the psychotherapeutic encounter, rather than on an extensive elaboration of the therapist's traditional interventive activities. However, it is equally impossible to propose an environment for psychotherapy that does not account for the verbal interaction between the two participants in the endeavor. For that reason I have attempted to capture this interaction in clinical vignettes, most of which contain examples of dialogue to illustrate the relational quality under discussion and the role that the psychotherapist's verbal interactivity plays in facilitating or hindering the development of this quality.

The construction of identity is fluid. Throughout the book I refer to the discovery/creation of an authentic self, because in the very act of discovering an aspect of oneself internally and then communicating that discovery to an external party, in this case the therapist, one *creates* identity (Spence 1982). The capacity to assert an internal discovery concerning one's identity adds to that identity. It is therefore impossible to propose that psychotherapy is simply a process of discovering one's identity (or anything else), as more traditional texts on psychotherapy, which emphasize the insight-producing or -uncovering activities of the therapist, might suggest. Instead, throughout this book psychotherapy is thought of as a truly dynamic and creative process.

OVERVIEW OF THE BOOK

The book is divided into two parts. The first briefly presents theoretical issues. Chapter Two argues that the primary difficulty that impels gay men to seek out a psychotherapist involves an alienation from the authentic self. The sociological and psychological determinants of this are reviewed. The concept of identity is explored from four complementary psychodynamic vantage points, that of Erikson's psychosocial model, Winnicott's object relations model, Sullivan's interpersonal model, and Kohut's self psychological model.

Chapter Three explores the goal of psychotherapy. In the traditional psychodynamic literature the goal of psychotherapy has often been considered to be changing the patient's life circumstances, thus relieving his distressing symptomatology. This is not an especially helpful model, however, when working with the gay man. The goal of psychotherapy with this patient, who has throughout his life received numerous calls to change, must be acceptance of his identity as he presents it. Paradoxically, when change is not the goal, symptomatological relief often does result from this endeavor. In this context, the concept of resistance is explored.

Part II presents clinical issues. Chapter Four focuses on the creation of a relational environment that facilitates acceptance and understanding of the patient's identity. Anonymity and neutrality are presented first. Anonymity, as it is often presented in the clinical literature, is argued to be a potential hindrance to the unfolding of psychotherapy if it is clung to tenaciously by the therapist. Instead, therapy is a process in which the full identities of both participants come to be known, whether acknowledged or not, and a rigid adherence to anonymity encourages the continuation of a patient's false self. Neutrality is proposed to be a stance of curiosity by the therapist toward the patient that precludes rigid judgments and stereotypes. One potential result of such a stance by the therapist is its adoption by the patient.

Chapter Five focuses on three additional qualities that must be present to allow the patient to discover/create his authentic self: respect—the therapist's unfailing attempts to maintain honesty with him- or herself and the patient; sensitivity—the therapist's acknowledgment that the patient is part of a larger sociocultural environment; and courtesy—the acclimation of the patient to the process of psychotherapy. Each of these qualities provides a symbolic experience for the patient that has been withheld by the larger culture because of his homosexuality.

Chapter Six concerns transference. The argument is offered that transference has two distinct, but coexistent, levels. The first is the compensatory level, in which the patient utilizes the therapist as a selfobject to compensate for deficits in his self structure. The second is the narrative level, in which the patient symbolically (generally verbally but through nonverbal communication as well) describes the specific state of affairs in his development that resulted in the self deficit(s). Transference is argued to be founded upon real qualities in the therapist and the roles of displacement and projection in transference are discussed as being of secondary importance.

Chapter Seven looks at countertransference and the involvement of the psychotherapist emotionally in the enterprise of psychotherapy. Countertransference is presented as the therapist's utilization of the patient as a selfobject that is ubiquitous but may have positive, negative, or neutral impact on the therapy. The concept of abstinence is explored as one that has often stifled the therapist's emotional involvement, especially for the novice therapist. The importance of the therapist's emotional involvement is highlighted as crucial to any conception of psychotherapy that emphasizes identity, as psychotherapy with gay men must.

Chapter Eight looks at the extensions of a psychotherapist's interest in authenticity outside his or her office. A patient's true interest in his own authentic identity kindles an interest in understanding the world around him in a more genuine way. Under such scrutiny the deceptions that guard discrimination are challenged. The psychotherapist is also challenged. The challenge to the psychotherapist is to become a social activist striving to make the culture more genuine, and thus more accepting of all differences, including homosexuality.

A FINAL NOTE

As a psychotherapist who is also a gay man, I have attempted to present a perspective on psychotherapy that respects the richness of psychodynamic theory development over the course of this century. However, I have also attempted to tailor it to the specific needs of one patient population with which I share a deep kinship. Because of this kinship, it is important to me that psychotherapy be a process that puts the best interests of the patient first. This has not always been, nor is always now, the case. The richness of dynamic theory (and the frank homophobia of some of its theorists and practitioners) has often led to rigid partisanship. Sometimes this partisanship has led to increased theoretical complexity—and decreased clinical utility. To put it more simply, we seem to have sometimes lost sight of the forest for the trees. Although there is no way to influence the fears and prejudices that a reader may bring to this book, it is possible to avoid adding to the convolution that has sometimes hindered effective responses to patients. Throughout the text I have tried to refrain from theoretical complexity in favor of clinical utility. My hope is that some gay men who seek dynamically informed psychotherapy may receive some benefit from this attempt.

2

Alienation from the Self: A Core Difficulty for Gay Men

Today, man is real only insofar as he is standing somewhere outside. He is constituted only through things, through property, through his social role, through his "persona"; as a living person, however, he is not real.

Erich Fromm

One of the things not expected of a tennis ball is that it should know it is a tennis ball.

R. D. Laing

THE MANY FACES OF ALIENATION

The difficulties that bring a gay man to psychotherapy can most often be understood as chronic and pervasive alienation from his internal life. Whether he describes it as a pervasive sense of emptiness, chronic boredom, depression, anxiety when alone, or as being unsure how he feels about important people in his life, he is articulating a difficulty in either achieving a coherent, integrated identity, asserting that identity, or, most often, both. The single most important difficulty that a gay man brings to a psychotherapist's office is in the area of identity.

Prior to consulting a therapist, the potential patient has already attempted to conceptualize what troubles him. In many cases the initial complaint concerns relationships. He deeply desires a relationship, but has been unable to find a suitable partner. If he has found a partner, he feels that the relationship is not working. In this instance he will generally blame himself for the relational difficulties, proposing that he is unskilled in the art of relationships. However, with exploration, it becomes easily apparent that the relationship does not meet his needs in a variety of ways. Yet, he holds himself responsible for all deficits in the relationship.

A patient may also come with the complaint that he is weary of compulsive sexual contacts that do not meet other than the most superficial of needs. In our current addiction-oriented culture, this lamentation often concerns what the patient may call "sexual addiction." Often, he is aware that part of this particular complaint involves a pervasive and chronic fear of being alone and a sense of boredom and/or anxiety when alone, but relegates these to a level of secondary importance.

Some gay men present with concerns about

AIDS. They may recently have discovered that they are seropositive for antibodies to HIV or that they have AIDS. In many cases they ascribe this physical infection to morally defective behavior. AIDS complicates the dynamic understanding of a gay man dramatically. Not only are there multiple issues of adaptation to the disease that require attention (e.g., mourning the loss of deteriorating physical capacities, accommodating to newly imposed physical and interpersonal limitations), but the disease itself often enacts the view the patient has of himself as morally defective. Some men almost seem relieved that they have been infected with the virus, as if they finally have a means of atoning for their "sinful" or "bad" lives (Hudson and Cornett 1993).

The same dynamic can be seen in gay men who are convinced that they are HIV positive or have AIDS with little or no corroborating data, or even in the face of contradictory evidence. Many patients that I have worked with are convinced that they have HIV infection even after multiple HIV antibody tests demonstrate no HIV seroconversion. Cabaj (1988) has identified an AIDS neurosis, phenomenologically and symptomatologically similar to classical compromise formation neuroses, which manifests itself as an obsessive belief that one has AIDS, culminating in physical symptoms resembling those seen in AIDS (or at least the patient's conception of AIDS) without underlying organic pathology.

Most gay men approach psychotherapy with deficits in their capacity to maintain durable, functional levels of self-esteem. In many cases they treat themselves with little empathy or are overtly punitive and pejorative toward themselves and the difficulties that gave impetus to the initial contact. As they describe their fears, anxieties, hopes, wishes, and feelings, self-attacks such as "stupid," "crazy," "neurotic," "weak," "sick," and a variety of others in varying degrees of subtlety are often used. They often hold themselves out as beyond understanding, certainly beyond empathic compassion. There is evident a deep wish to be understood along with a deep fear that they will be hurt.

Gay men often present with a deep and abiding contempt for their own feelings. Over the last ten years, a large majority of the gay men that I have worked with have devalued their pain, sadness, or anger by making comparisons to "other people" who have it "a lot worse." They deride themselves for feeling pain about their life circumstances when there are others who are physically disabled, without food, and so on. If one listens carefully, the voice of an unempathic parental and cultural milieu makes itself undeniably clear.

Many who work primarily with heterosexual men and women can identify their own patients in this description as well. The tendency to treat oneself with little regard has not confined itself to the gay subculture. Indeed, a lack of empathy toward the self and others has reached epidemic proportions in this culture (Miller 1981). However, disregard for the self, whether called internalized homophobia, shame, self-loathing, or self-hatred, seems to figure prominently in the lives of large numbers of gay men. There are a variety of ways to conceptualize this phenomenon, but all of them are founded on difficulties in the establishment of a basic identity structure.

THE SEARCH FOR IDENTITY
AND CULTURAL DYNAMICS

Over forty years ago existential dynamic clinicians began to observe identity difficulties in Western culture. May (1953) proposed that the core difficulty facing a large number of people in this and other Western countries was an internal void that created a palpable sense of emptiness or hollowness. People were alienated from the core feelings, values, and beliefs that could define their individuality. May proposed that, for the mid–twentieth century person, the goal of life was not to form a unique identity that defined one as distinct from others, but had instead become the achievement of a pseudo-identity that reflected those qualities that were accepted and popular throughout the larger society. The symmetry that could be achieved through many distinct identities pulling the social fabric in multiple directions had been supplanted by conformity to a form of social ideal. May describes this in regard to the tendency of individuals to subordinate their assessment of the value of a course of action to the judgments of an external, social audience:

> It is as though one had always to postpone his judgment until he looked at his audience. The person who is passive, to whom or for whom the act is done, has the power to make the act effective or ineffective, rather than the one who is doing it. Thus we tend to be *performers* in life rather than persons who live and act as selves. [p.60]

May's work, like that of Fromm (1956, 1969), was based on the rich traditions of both psychoanalysis and existentialism, as well as a keen interest in the effects of the social and cultural milieu on the individual (May 1983).

European existentialism had long been concerned with the capacity of the person to develop a realization of the values that constitute the nucleus of identity. Sartre (1957) was particularly concerned with the relationship between the discovery or realization of internal values and the ultimate pattern into which one's life could be organized. This pattern, predicated upon the most intimate of one's values, gave expression to one's belief of what constitutes meaning in life. The combined realization of values and the enactment of these in the pursuit of meaning imbued each person with a unique identity. The existentialist "thinks that man, with no support and no aid, is condemned every moment to invent man" (p. 23). However, like May, many of the existential thinkers concluded that for many, if not most, people the central value of life becomes acceptance and the pursuit of popularity becomes the organizing meaning of life.

Psychoanalysis, too, was born through a desire to help patients reach an understanding of their core being. The Victorian age was a repressive one. Sexuality was especially taboo. People were expected to divorce themselves from their sexuality or to behave as if they had successfully done so. If they were actually successful in the repudiation of their sexuality, they developed the conversion symptoms typical of many of Freud's early patients. If the latter path was chosen, they lived a double life—one purporting to exhibit the most virtuous of morals (e.g., the repudiation of sex) and another in which the baser instincts reigned, albeit usually guiltily. Robert Louis Stevenson's *Dr. Jekyll and Mr. Hyde* symbolically exemplifies this compromise with a social structure that bred hypocrisy.

Bettelheim (1982) believed that Freud's work was deeply concerned with the broadest context of human identity development. Indeed, he argues strongly that the terms that have become standard descriptors in psychoanalytic ego psychology—id, ego, and superego—are far removed from Freud's original intent. The soul (in the German, *seele*) was the focus of Freud's interest and psychoanalysis was developed as a means of helping patients develop a complete and integrated identity.

However, May (1953) asserts that Freud's life and work preceded the age of emptiness that characterizes the modern human being. He is, to a certain extent, correct in that assertion. Freud's work does focus on alienation from the self, but it is a rather circumscribed alienation he describes. Freud's emphasis was on lifting the repressive barriers that blocked full integration of sexuality into the self. He does not describe the vast emptiness and fragmentation of general identity that characterize many people today. Primarily this seems to be because, although Victorian society was repressive in the values it prescribed and proscribed, it offered a structure against which one could define the self.

Twentieth-century Western culture has evolved past Victorian standards of identity. This has brought increased freedom, but with it a greater confusion and a greater propensity toward identity fragmentation. Silverstein (1993) comments on the implications of this state of affairs for the gay man. He proposes that the identity confusion, diffusion, and fragmentation characteristic of the borderline personality disorder (BPD) may be useful metaphorically in understanding the lack of a coherent, integrated identity that is often the foundation for difficulties in gay men's lives.

Silverstein (1993) cites the massive social changes of the past fifty years, including the women's and gay liberation movements and the diminution of religious domination in life, as offering people more choices about the values they embrace and ultimately the directions their identities take. However, along with the freedom and the increased choices available to everyone in Western culture, but perhaps especially gay men, have also come greater opportunities for identity confusion and fragmentation.

> Individuals are now forced to make a considerable number of choices over sexual behavior, sexual identity, and gender. It is a task wherein a person is asked to create order out of confusion, and from that ordering of personal and social alternatives evolves a psychological structure that is the modern equivalent of rules from, say, the Victorian era, . . . the most important responsibility for each person in today's society is to create this personal psychological structure as a replacement for the former social and religious regulations. [p. 126]

THE SEARCH FOR IDENTITY: FOUR PSYCHOANALYTIC FORMULATIONS

Although this book will ultimately focus on Kohut's (1977, 1984) self psychology as an explanatory theory, it is important to describe the work of three other theorists who have influenced the current psychoanalytic understanding of identity formation and development: Erikson (1963, 1982), Winnicott (1965), and Sullivan (1953, 1954). In understanding the gay man all four of these approaches are of value.

Erik Erikson and the Psychosocial Conception of Identity

Erikson (1963) was the first of the psychoanalytic developmental theorists to focus on both identity development and the importance of adulthood in psychological life. He noted that "the study of identity . . . becomes as strategic in our time as the study of sexuality was in Freud's time" (p. 282). Erikson specifically proposed adolescence to be a time of identity formation and solidification (or diffusion). Erikson's model was unique because it proposed that development is influenced by psychosocial forces. The human being does not develop in a vacuum or in a world populated only by parents, although they are obviously of critical importance.

Instead, Erikson noted that identity is influenced by a variety of cultural, symbolic, and social factors. Of primary significance in the growing person's life is his interaction with the people and activities of his society that symbolically or in actuality confirm his identity. One simple example is dating. The heterosexual adolescent is supported in his or her attempts to attract members of the opposite sex. Adults and peers offer hints (although not always helpful) as to how to most successfully achieve this. There are

symbolic events designed to support the dating heterosexual adolescent, like school dances and proms.

Malyon (1993) points out the immediate importance of this for the gay man. Ours is a heterosexually
oriented culture. It confirms heterosexual identity in
myriad subtle and more blatant ways. From the col-
lusive wink of a father or other male to intimate discussions of the meaning of love and relationships in
life, the adolescent receives a great deal of direction
and confirmation of what it means to be a heterosexual male in our culture. This is not the case with the
gay male adolescent. Indeed, there are no rituals, activities, or rites of passage that confirm a gay man's
identity. The ritual of dating again illustrates this. For
example, thousands of adolescents attend school
proms, and other than family pictures and an occasional brief newspaper blurb, there is seldom any special notice taken of this ritual. However, when a
homosexual male adolescent escorts a male date to a
prom as Aaron Fricke (1981) did some years ago, it
makes national headlines. It also raises legal questions that never confront the heterosexual adolescent.

A homosexual adolescent is expected to adapt
the heterosexual vehicles of identity confirmation to
his own needs, without instruction on how to do so or
even acknowledgment that adaptation is necessary.
He is also expected to do so secretly. If he is not totally
successful in achieving this adaptation, an overwhelming task indeed, the result is generally deficits
in his identity confirmation. Malyon (1993) proposes
that these deficits, along with the resulting difficulties in establishing intimate bonds based on differentiation of self from others, create much havoc in gay
men's intimate, especially romantic, relationships.

He likens psychotherapy with gay men to an endeavor often focused on aiding them in developing beyond a search for identity confirmation, a developmental task often achieved by heterosexuals during adolescence.

Interestingly, many psychotherapists point to this phenomenon as evidence that gay men are inherently pathological, with no acknowledgment that solidification of one's identity, a formidable task under the best of conditions, is significantly more difficult for the gay man. Although Erikson did not address the developmental tasks and phenomena specific to the gay man, his psychosocial developmental schema provides amply for the important role that society plays in the establishment and maintenance of identity. It is also a theory that provides important elements for understanding the gay man throughout adulthood (Cornett and Hudson 1987).

Harry Stack Sullivan: Reflected Appraisals

Sullivan was also concerned with the formation and development of identity. By some accounts himself a homosexual and the product of an isolated and lonely childhood, Sullivan was keenly aware of the role that the interpersonal environment plays in the development of identity:

> It is in the months of infancy and the years of childhood that the principal changes are wrought by which an animal with an ultraelaborate apparatus for communal existence and within extremely complex situations is caused to take on the peculiar features

subsumed in man as a creature of culture—in the
human individual as a *person*. [Sullivan 1965, p. 41]

Sullivan (1953) asserted that the unique personality
of each individual—his identity—is determined in
large part by the appraisals of others around him. He
stressed that these appraisals can both facilitate
growth and serve as the foundation of psychological
difficulties. In Sullivan's work anxiety particularly is
linked with the expectation of rejection or being
assessed as inadequate: "Anxiety, as a phenomenon
of relatively adult life, can often be explained plau-
sibly as anticipated unfavorable appraisal of one's
current activity by someone whose opinion is significant" (p. 113).

For the homosexual man this perspective is often
particularly useful in its explanatory power of the
symptomatology pushing him to psychotherapy. It
proposes that identity is influenced by the interpersonal reactions of others to the identity presented. In
modern Western culture the presentation of a homosexual identity is seldom met with more than condi-
tional acceptance. More often, the presentation of a
homosexual identity is met with contempt, rejection,
and derision. The subtleties and pervasiveness of this
phenomenon are illustrated by a young patient who
described an early memory of watching a television
program with his family that contained an incidental,
but pejorative, reference to male homosexuality. He
remembered knowing intuitively that it was *his*
sexual orientation to which the program referred,
although he could neither have defined nor described
what was meant by the term. He remembered feeling
anxious and a little nauseated as he contemplated the

negative connotations of the program's treatment of homosexuality. However, what he most remembered was the cold terror of hearing his father comment on his disappointment that "there are *those* kinds of people in the world" and his mother's enthusiastic assent.

This is a mild experience compared to the overt rejections that are encountered by the homosexual boy and man throughout his life. In Sullivan's terms, negative appraisals of the homosexual identity emanate from a variety of sources and must be confronted by the developing gay man on an almost continual basis. Politicians, religious leaders, and even some psychotherapists condemn homosexuality as "un-American," an enemy of "family values," "sinful," "perverse," or "pathological." However, the common sobriquets that are hurled on the streets are even more pointed—terms like "faggot," "fairy," and "cock-sucker."

Some argue that these experiences of rejection are no more extensive or qualitatively different than the rejections faced by large numbers of other people who are members of racial or ethnic minority groups. There is one vast difference, however, between the rejections that these groups face and the rejections that are a part of the lives of homosexual men. Members of racial and ethnic groups that face hatred and rejection on that basis can be virtually assured of not being rejected within their own families. Gay men have no such guarantee and the majority of gay men face some emotional or physical rejection when they assert their identities to their families (Kimmel 1978).

From the perspective of Sullivan's conception of identity, as involving the internalization of the as-

sessments, evaluations, and descriptions of significant others, the miasma of contempt in which the gay
man develops is of crucial importance. It offers important information in explaining the sense of emptiness that many gay men complain of as therapy
begins. It also offers information on the hunger for
relationships that gay men manifest with the paradoxical anxiety in accepting relational intimacy once
it has been offered. Bombarded by negative evaluations all their lives, many gay men internalize representations of themselves as inadequate or morally
bad. However, there is also a realization that there is
no other way to be. The only compromise available in
many cases is to maintain an alienation from the self.
Integration of feelings is especially minimized because the result of complete integration would be
overwhelming confrontation with the self that is so
hated by the larger society. In the logical extreme this
alienation represents the complete break that characterizes many schizophrenic episodes. The need to
sacrifice a homosexual identity at any cost, including
a schizophrenic break, was of deep interest to Sullivan (1962) and his work in this area made his initial
reputation.

Alienation from the self can also be expressed
interpersonally. A gay man may often talk about a
desire for a romantic relationship. He will search and
yearn for the partner who will make him feel loved
and accepted. However, when he does find a partner
who cares about him, this experience can only be
enjoyed briefly. Soon a number of disappointments in
the partner make themselves known and he finds
himself increasingly distant from the relationship.
When explored, this pattern reveals first a lack of

conviction that the man originally searching for love truly deserves it, and second that the person found is deeply suspect because he is also homosexual. One patient quoted Groucho Marx when describing this phenomenon: "I don't care to belong to a club that accepts people like me as members."

Donald W. Winnicott and the False Self

Winnicott (1965) was also intensely interested in the development of identity. Like Sullivan, he wrote about the outcome of identity development when a child faces a hostile environment, one either overtly rejecting of him or one in which the primary caregivers are narcissistically impaired in such a way that they cannot tolerate the child asserting a unique identity.

From a Kleinian foundation, Winnicott built much of his theory of the development of the self on the concept of splitting. The child, in response to cues obtained from caregivers, attempts to split off aspects of the self that are displeasing to them. He attempts to maintain an identity characterized only by qualities that he believes they find acceptable and lovable.

Caregivers positively recognize a child's compliance in meeting their expectations in a variety of ways. The child learns that compliance with the caregivers' wishes and expectations brings acceptance and love. As he develops, the child becomes exquisitely sensitive to the nuances of caregivers' expectations. He strives to meet these as often as possible. In many instances, one expectation of narcissistically well-developed parents is that the child grow into his own unique potential. However, if the child's primary caregivers are empty themselves, Winnicott observed, then one overpowering expectation can be that the child fulfill their narcissistic needs, thereby denying his own. One aspect of this drama is the expectation by caregivers that the child think, feel, and behave as they do. They demand that the child subjugate his authentic wishes, feelings, desires, thoughts, and behavior to those that they would find more satisfying.

Compliance with the demand to give up the authenticity of the internal world leads to the development of a false self (Winnicott 1965). The false self is initially an interpersonal posture that gradually becomes an intrapersonal structure. The natural and understandable striving for caregiver acceptance, approval, and affirmation gradually comes to alienate the child from his own internal world. Moore and Fine (1990c) liken the false self to imposture and stress that it can serve as a means of deceiving others, "serving defensive, integrative, narcissistic, and self-cohesive functions, as well as gratifying instinctual drives" (p. 93). While this is true, it is important to note that the foremost dynamic of the false self is *self-deception* in order to gain the acceptance and approval of others rather than for sociopathic purposes.

Winnicott's explanation of the false self illuminates one dynamic underlying more existentially and sociologically oriented psychoanalysts' (e.g., Fromm 1969, May 1953) observations of our culture as one built upon conformity. It also adds another important component to the understanding of a homosexual man's identity.

Isay (1989) proposes that an important dynamic of homosexual development is the resolution of an oedipal conflict. However, he begins with the assumption that, for homosexual boys, this conflict is played out in relation to a desire for the father. He, as well as others (Friedman 1988, Green 1987), have proposed that the young homosexual boy may take on characteristics that he believes might interest the father. These can include sensitivity and other qualities traditionally assigned to the female. However, rather than interest the father, these qualities often frighten and repel him, perhaps both because of the homoerotic aspects of the boy's presentation and because of the extreme difficulty many men have in integrating their own feminine qualities. As a result, the boy experiences a great deal of rejection from his father, leading to severe narcissistic injury. This may be compounded by rejections in various ways, including sexual exploitation by other males in his life (Friedman 1990).

In response to these painful experiences of rejection, many homosexual boys reject the offending part of their identities. They essentially develop a false self based on what they come to understand as their fathers' expectations. For many boys this includes a denial of their homosexuality well into adulthood. Heterosexual marriage can be one form that this denial takes. A staunch reaction formation against all things homoerotic can be another. Even for those men who acknowledge their homosexuality, there can be an almost phobic revulsion to any feeling, mannerism, or characteristic that is deemed effeminate.

The double life led by deeply "closeted" men can

be understood in this light. While it is certainly true that a number of factors combine to sustain a closeted life, none is probably more important in explaining it than Winnicott's concept of the false self. It provides the clearest explanation of why a homosexual man would carry out complicated and intricate activities of deception to sustain a particular job rather than simply seeking a job in his field with an employer more accepting of gay men.

Finally, the false self offers some understanding of the motivations underlying efforts at sexual reorientation psychotherapy. Rather than integrate the feelings, thoughts, fantasies, and behaviors that constitute homosexuality into their larger identity, some men search out psychotherapists purporting to "cure" homosexuality. Such psychotherapists make use of the false self to keep such patients alienated from their authentic internal worlds. Psychotherapists who might generally maintain the inviolability of therapeutic neutrality with other patients, violate neutrality with homosexual men. Examples of this include offering advice on heterosexual dating and sexual behavior (Socarides 1978) and prohibiting homosexual behavior while under treatment (A. Freud 1954). Such deviations from attempting to understand to attempting to manipulate are best understood as techniques for strengthening a weakening false self and limiting a true one.

With some homosexual men these strategies fall temporarily on fertile ground. The desperation to be loved and accepted is a powerful motivation. However, many, after "successful" analyses or psychotherapies focused on changing their identities, ultimately find their way to an analyst or therapist who is more interested in discovering and liberating their true selves than suppressing them. Clinical work in such second attempts, however, is generally complicated by the often severe damage done in the first treatment (Isay 1993a).

Heinz Kohut and Self Psychology

Self psychology has also been intimately concerned with identity development. With his abiding interest in the developmental line followed by narcissism, Kohut (1971, 1977) made self-esteem a centerpiece of his theory of the development of identity.

Kohut recognized that the maintenance of a cohesive, integrated identity is predicated on the capacity to maintain functional levels of self-esteem in the face of narcissistic injury. Identity is dependent on the ability of the person to soothe himself in the face of disappointment. If one cannot maintain a sufficient level of self-esteem in the face of a disappointing or otherwise painful situation, one is prone to fragmentation experiences. Such experiences are moments of identity disruption. They are characteristically subjectively perceived as moments of being overwhelmed, depersonalized, and derealized, and experiencing a lack of contact with what is truly felt or thought.

Self-esteem also plays an obvious role in asserting oneself. Functional levels of self-esteem sustain one not only in the face of narcissistic injury, but also in the face of moments of pride or assertion. If one does not feel adequate to recognition or praise, then moments of compliment or acknowledgment can be opportunities for fragmentation. Evidence of this type of fragmentation abounds. It is not at all uncommon to witness someone become embarrassed, flustered, and almost panicked after receiving a compliment.

Difficulty in asserting oneself is a similar phenomenon. One encounters it in innumerable mundane situations. Someone is asked where he or she would like to go for lunch and responds, "I don't care, wherever you want to go." Even after being pressed, it seems impossible for the person to assert a preference. Where to have lunch is a minor life decision; the difficulty in asserting oneself can be much more threatening in situations with higher stakes. Such situations offer the opportunity for fragmentation as well. Miller (1981), who has done much to bring both Winnicott's and Kohut's thinking to a wider popular audience, describes the importance of self-esteem in identity very succinctly: "[One] knows not only what he does not want but also what he wants and is able to express this, irrespective of whether he will be loved or hated for it" (p. 33).

Kohut (1977, 1984) recognized that the development and maintenance of self-esteem occur in an interpersonal milieu. Through interaction with self-objects, initially the primary caregivers, the child develops the rudimentary capacity to soothe himself. Kohut delineated three primary selfobject functions served initially by the parents:

1. Through mirroring, the parents reflect the developing child's grandiosity. They acknowledge his attempts at autonomous functioning, creativity, and so on, and in this way prepare the child to be able to tolerate moments of accomplishment and pride, as

well as to comfort himself during moments of disappointment.

2. By allowing the child to idealize them the parents lend the child their strength in moments of distress. The parents are perceived by the child as stronger and more competent than he. Through idealization he can merge with that strength and competence, thus providing a calming reassurance when faced with difficulties or threats.

3. Through their twinship functions, caregivers offer the child a connection to the rest of humanity. As a part of the human community the child can feel a part of a larger entity during times of distress. He is not isolated in his troubles; others have faced and are facing similar difficulties. The twinship selfobject sphere not only militates against a sense of isolation in the face of threat, it provides a sense of responsibility to the larger human community.

Self psychology is very helpful in understanding many gay men who seek psychotherapy. Because of difficulties in maintaining self-esteem, they are prone to severe fragmentation in the face of slights or other narcissistic injuries. Many are unable to set limits or maintain boundaries with others who treat them abusively. Similarly, moments of recognition for achievement elicit shame rather than pride. Indeed, pride is often a threatening feeling state. The desire for recognition and affirmation are deemed morally reprehensible. Many have a great deal of difficulty in soothing themselves in the face of disappointment. Because identity boundaries are not solid, they have difficulty in merging with idealized others to provide a sense of strength and protection while simultaneously maintaining a separate identity. Finally, they often feel isolated in relation to the rest of humanity. Distress common to the human condition is often related to homosexuality and therefore beyond the comforting realization that some travails of life are endemic to simply being a mortal.

For the gay man, selfobjects are often faulty. Not only does a gay man face the inevitable traumata that are a part of growing up with fallible caregivers, he faces narcissistic injuries specific to being homosexual in a heterosexual culture. The relationship with his father, discussed earlier, is often the first faulty selfobject relationship. If the boy intuitively senses his father's rejection because of his differentness, one potential source of mirroring is compromised. Similarly, rejection by the father may close an opportunity to merge with the father's strength in idealization and to feel connected to him as another male in the twinship selfobject sphere.

Compounding this difficult situation is the fact that, for the heterosexual boy, there are a variety of people and activities that can serve selfobject functions in the larger culture if the father is inadequate. However, there are no activities for boys in our culture that are not predicated on heterosexuality. Scouting is an excellent example of this.

The Boy Scouts of America serves a remarkably important function in the lives of many boys. Through the scouting experience boys become a part of a larger group and are able to connect their identities as males to other males, both peers and adults (i.e., the twinship selfobject function). Through interaction with the adult leaders, the boys are taught and master basic skills in a variety of areas. As they do so they are awarded merit badges and receive mirroring responses from the adults and other boys. They also, again through interaction with the adult volunteers, receive the opportunity to idealize and internalize aspects of these men that they might ultimately want to incorporate into their own identities.

However, this scenario is not as available to the homosexual boy. First, the Boy Scouts of America currently forbids openly gay men to be adult leaders. (This seems to be, at least in part, the result of stereotypic confusion between homosexuality and pedophilia.) Therefore there are no men like the homosexual boy to develop in response to or resonance with. If there are gay men involved with the organization, they are generally, of necessity, deeply closeted. The homosexual boy in this instance experiences interaction with a false self and is thus encouraged to strengthen his own false self. Further, there are covert, if not blatantly overt, criticisms of homosexuality in the code of moral conduct of the scouting tradition. So the experience, that for a heterosexual boy can be affirming and solidifying because of its inherent opportunities to experience pride, idealization, and camaraderie, offers to the homosexual boy opportunities for shame, self-denigration, and alienation from his core identity.

It is also worth noting that scouting, although much publicized currently because of its stand on homosexuality (and because it is an organization that holds so much potential for *every* boy), is not the exception, but rather the rule. There are no consistent symbols, rituals, institutions, or organizations that are accessible to large numbers of homosexual boys.

SUMMARY

My contention about dynamically oriented psychotherapy with gay men is a simple one; to be successful it must be focused on creating an environment that aids the patient in discovering/ creating and affirming an identity that is often treated as anathema in our culture. This form of psychotherapy encourages the patient to seek discovery of the true self, generally buried beneath layers of culturally fostered self-deception, and then offers a relationship that affirms that true self. The chapters that follow present the perspective and activities of the psychotherapist that facilitate these tasks. A psychotherapeutic experience that offers a gay man this opportunity offers him not only a new relationship with himself, but the potential to find a relationship in his interpersonal environment that is affirming and accepting.

3

Reconsidering the Goal of Psychotherapy

Any technique concerned with the other without the self, with behavior to the exclusion of experience, with the relationship to the neglect of the persons in relation, with the individuals to the exclusion of their relationship, and most of all, with an object-to-be-changed rather than a person-to-be-accepted, simply perpetuates the disease it purports to cure.

R. D. Laing

All [psychiatric] diagnoses are driven by non-medical, that is, economic, personal, legal, political, or social considerations and incentives.

Thomas Szasz

PATIENT CHANGE AS A GOAL

Discussions of psychotherapeutic technique often focus extensively on the activities of the psychotherapist without overt reference to the goals of the enterprise. There may be cursory discussions of broad goals (e.g., establishing the supremacy of the ego in the tripartite structure of the mind), but the most basic goal of psychotherapy is almost universally assumed—to ameliorate the patient's suffering. To achieve this goal it is also assumed that the psychotherapist must facilitate change in the patient and, through this change, bring about an internal, subjective sense of relief and an external, perhaps objective, reduction in symptomatology. (Throughout this chapter, the term *change* is used in its broadest and most generic sense, not to mean the replacement of homosexuality with heterosexuality, often referred to as "change therapy.") Schafer (1983) defines *analytic help* as "the help that is offered . . . in understanding one's past and present life more fully in order to be able to change oneself for the better" (p. 11).

The primary goal of psychotherapy is generally conceived to be a result—improvement (i.e., change) in the patient's life—rather than as a process. To be as helpful as possible to the gay male patient, a psychotherapist should disabuse him- or herself of this conception. The goal of helping a patient to change in order to relieve his distress has a number of factors working actively against it. Chiefly, this goal militates against the patient discovering/creating his own identity. Instead, it sets an externally derived paradigm of identity predicated on notions of *health* and *dysfunction* (Isay 1993a). No matter how it is conceptualized, a paradigm that supposes that the product of psychotherapy is change has significant assumptions as to the foundations on which identity should be built.

The vast majority of psychotherapists wish to help their patients with the distress in their lives. Even if not initially, most clinicians come to care, often deeply, about their patients. The psychotherapist wishes to relieve the patient's suffering. This wish forms an essential part of the foundation upon which helpful psychotherapy is constructed. It often, though not invariably, coincides with the patient's wishes for the outcome of the psychotherapy. However, an equally strong wish of the patient is to avoid change and the disruptive effects that change can bring to his identity (Castelnuovo-Tedesco 1989, Gay 1989). As Fromm (1989) proposes, patients primarily "pretend" to want to change. The clinician's wish to ameliorate the patient's suffering must be tempered by the patient's fear of change. For this reason, change in the patient is best relegated to a secondary goal of any treatment. In short, the psychotherapist's desire to aid the patient is most helpful if it is part of a conceptual context that guards against this desire becoming the entirety or dominant aspect of the process.

This chapter explores an alternative to viewing the goal of psychotherapy as principally involving change, and instead views its goal as the creation of an ambiance that offers the patient an experience that is his to embrace or reject. In this conceptualization, change, if it occurs at all, is a by-product of this experience, not its goal.

DIAGNOSIS AND ASSESSMENT

Diagnosis is a cornerstone of the implementation of the therapist's values regarding health and illness in the pursuit of change. Diagnosis in its most basic medical sense concerns the discovery of the etiology of a pathological condition so that a treatment regimen can be implemented to ameliorate the condition. It is as simple as discovering that a patient has a bacterial infection so that antibiotics can be prescribed to resolve the infection, or discovering that a patient has an operable malignancy so that a surgical strategy can be arrived at to remove it. There are many advantages and few disadvantages to this type of medical diagnosis. However, because psychoanalysis and dynamic psychotherapy, at least in this country, have historically been principally the domain of physicians, diagnosis has also found its way into psychotherapeutic practice, where its disadvantages are many and its advantages few.

Menninger and colleagues (1963) propose that psychodynamic diagnosis is

> diagnosis in the sense of understanding just how the patient is ill and how ill the patient is, how he became ill and how his illness serves him. From this knowledge one may draw logical conclusions regarding how changes might be brought about in or around the patient which would affect his illness. [pp. 6–7]

The disadvantages of diagnosis in psychotherapeutic practice fall primarily in the effect that diagnosis has on the clinician's a priori understanding of the patient's identity (and, as Menninger and colleagues suggest, how it should be changed). First, diagnosis in the psychological realm often becomes a descriptor of the totality of the patient's identity. Gabbard (1990) stresses that a psychotherapist, after completing a psychodynamic assessment, should formulate both a descriptive and a psychodynamic diagnosis: "Both diagnoses inform the treatment planning, but the descriptive diagnosis is geared toward the assignment of the correct label, the latter is viewed as a summary of understanding that goes beyond the label" (p. 61).

One obvious set of corollary difficulties presents itself from this conception of diagnosis. First, no label will ever be sophisticated enough to encompass the nuances of an entire person. People are much too complex to ever be adequately categorized. The elegance of life is predicated upon this complexity and reductionistic diagnostic labels, by their very nature, devalue this complexity and elegance.

The second difficulty that Gabbard (1990) acknowledges is that a thorough understanding of the person comes about through psychotherapy, not prior to it. An accurate diagnosis is only realistically possible at the conclusion of a course of psychotherapy, if then. Diagnosis does not precede treatment, but instead, follows it.

Also, psychological diagnosis often becomes a means of expressing negative feelings or, more traditionally, countertransference (see Chapter Seven) toward a patient (Cornett 1993c, Fine 1982). Most diagnoses take on a pejorative, even morally judgmental, connotation when bandied about by therapists. One has only to listen briefly to a group of therapists to hear patients called "borderline," "schizophrenic," "obsessive," and so on. Under such circumstances a patient ceases to be a complicated and rich creature seeking understanding and becomes an object that is understood a priori, albeit understood in the context of the therapist's value system regarding health and illness (Isay 1993a). For the therapist, the identity of the patient becomes synonymous with an illness, and, whether intended or not, this negatively influences how much freedom is offered to the patient to discover/create his true self. Further, negative emotional reactions toward the patient expressed in this manner are less prone to be seen by the clinician as an acting-out phenomenon. The rage, hate, and fear covered by diagnostic labels employed pejoratively are often not addressed by the clinician. This not only interferes in the clinician's ability to respond sensitively and empathically to the patient, but enacts a facade, a professional false self, that encourages the patient to retain an inauthentic identity.

It is worth noting that the general medical practitioner can arrive at a diagnosis with much more assurance and precision than can a psychotherapist. Staphylococcus bacteria are either present or they are not. If they are present, two trained physicians will see them as staphylococcus bacteria. The same is not true with psychiatric diagnoses. What constitutes a symptom, how many symptoms form constellations, and how many symptom constellations form disorders are somewhat subjective issues and the product of interpretation. Two trained psychotherapists may or may not see a phenomenon as a symptom, and if they concur that a phenomenon *is* a symptom, they may or may not agree on the diagnosis it merits. This is illustrated by contact with patients who have seen a number of different therapists.

One gay man who had seen a variety of psycho-therapists and psychiatrists brought a list of over twenty diagnoses he had received over the years to his first appointment with me. These diagnoses covered a broad range, from paranoid schizophrenia to schizoaffective disorder to major depression and obsessive-compulsive disorder.

Grown accustomed to having his identity defined by others, he asked me at the end of our first hour, "Well, what do you think I am?"

My first response, "You seem to be expecting me to label you, *as if* that would really help me understand you," met with a renewed demand to hear me voice a diagnostic label.

He pressed again, "Well? What do you say? What do you think I am?"

"A person," I replied quietly. This response, and my subsequent refusal to label him as "sick" at first disappointed him and gave him pause to question my expertise. However, as his therapy progressed, this response was repeatedly returned to as an important moment of acceptance and affirmation of him as unique, someone who could not be quickly and dismissively understood.

Adding to the unreliability of psychiatric diagnosis is its status as a fundamentally political entity (Laing 1971, Morgan and Nerison 1993, Szasz 1994a). As Bayer (1981) notes, homosexuality was a psychiatric diagnosis until 1974. A vote of the board of directors of the American Psychiatric Association, followed by a national referendum of the membership of that organization, removed it from the official list of mental disorders. Diagnoses that can be used, however well intentioned, to define a person's identity and are subject to a vote are inherently dangerous (Szasz 1994a).

Gay men are particularly wary of diagnoses. Although they often label themselves pejoratively (and often invoke pseudopsychological terms to do so), the process of a therapist assigning a diagnosis is painful because it is symbolically representative of the dismissive and narcissistically injurious treatment received from the heterosexual culture. Often, a gay man's diagnosis of himself with harsh terminology has a defensive aspect. It serves as a preemptive strike against the self, or, in ego psychological terms, an identification with the aggressor.

A diagnosis is another means of definition based on an incomplete picture of the man involved. After all, the term *homosexual* (or more abusive sobriquets) is used as a means of identifying and defining the totality of a man, based on his *difference* from the larger culture. As differences are treated with fear and contempt in our culture, such an identification or definition is threatening indeed.

Diagnosis offers any patient an opportunity for rejection. Beyond providing little, if any, useful information to the clinician, a diagnostic label often erects a barrier beyond which understanding does not pass. Freud (1937) proposed the use of diagnosis as a means of ascertaining the analyzability of a patient. In the early psychoanalytic diagnostic schema, only neuroses were amenable to psychoanalytic treatment. Entire groups of people, including male homosexuals, were considered too impaired to benefit from analysis. As psychoanalytic clinical theory has developed, such distinctions have come increasingly to be seen as arbitrary and limiting. Despite the best intentions, labeling and typologizing interfere in the process of understanding the unique nuances of each individual life.

I am not suggesting that in our imperfect world diagnoses are never needed for insurance forms and so on. However, the use of mild diagnoses with the sole goal of aiding a patient in obtaining insurance reimbursement is very different from the belief that a diagnosis actually imparts useful clinical information. The former is a *relatively* harmless artifact of practicing psychotherapy in a commercial environment. The latter, however, is a not-so-harmless artifact of an attempt to place psychotherapy in the realm of "medical science"—an environment that is not conducive to understanding a person in toto.

ASSESSMENT OVER DIAGNOSIS

Gabbard (1990) notes that diagnosis may be helpful in deciding on psychopharmacological intervention or hospitalization. However, he does not divorce diagnosis from assessment. *Assessment* can be an invaluable aid to treatment, but it need not—and to be helpful should not—result in a diagnosis.

A dynamic assessment offers the clinician important information about the patient. Primarily, it offers her/him information on courses of action that could potentially be of benefit. For instance, would the patient potentially benefit from medication? Hospitalization? Are there environmental modifications that could help with the patient's difficulties (e.g., for a man living with AIDS who has no physician, would referral to a physician be helpful? Would referral to a support group be helpful?). Are there other people who may need to be involved in the patient's care? A thoughtful assessment, which explores the patient's history and current life circumstances, can answer these questions. Additionally, an assessment can strengthen the identity of the patient.

Sullivan (1954) notes that a thoughtful dynamic assessment can strengthen a patient's identity by placing him in a context of history and development. For reasons outlined in the previous chapter, many gay patients come to a psychotherapist's office without a clear sense of themselves as *actors* in the drama of their lives. Indeed, although it is not consciously considered, nor easily articulated, they often see themselves as buffeted about by the whims of others or malevolent impersonal forces. This is a natural outgrowth of the multiple assaults on their narcissistic and identity development throughout their lives. They also often have difficulty in seeing themselves as historically grounded. Because there is an alienation from their identity, there is also an alienation from a sense of historical continuity.

A skillful assessment can begin a patient thinking of himself as a product of historical and contemporary developmental phenomena, feelings, thoughts, and actions. Simply by confirming a patient as part of a continuous historical and developmental process, the therapist offers him the opportunity to see himself as the source of action in the drama of his life rather than simply a diversionary character.

Although maintaining the assessment as a part of the diagnostic process, Schafer (1983) articulates this aspect of an assessment well. He argues against language that makes the patient a passive participant in his life (e.g., pathology, symptom, cure) and likens the process of assessment, and more broadly, the entire treatment experience, to a search for clarification and understanding that offers the patient an increased sense of control over his life.

> Increasingly during this process, the "patient" will present apparent demonic forces and unyielding structures as personal actions and begin to live his . . . life less painfully, apprehensively, self-deceptively, and unintelligibly. The "patient" will construct other and better situations to live in and will do so with an enhanced and more rational sense of personal responsibility. [p. 112]

RESISTANCE AND RECONCEPTUALIZING THE ULTIMATE GOAL OF PSYCHOTHERAPY

If the goal of psychotherapy with gay men is not change, two questions present themselves: What *is* the goal of psychotherapy? How does the concept of resistance fit into such a conceptualization? We start with an exploration of the second question, which may help elucidate the first.

Resistance

As was alluded to previously, patients in psychoanalysis and dynamic psychotherapy fear change (Castelnuovo-Tedesco 1989, Gay 1989). In the traditional psychoanalytic conception of treatment, resistance has been conceptualized as a patient's efforts to avoid change. Fundamentally, however, resistance to change was also seen as the reluctance to give up a symptom or illness that offered secondary gains. Resistances have been conceptualized as obstacles to treatment, to be moved past in order to resolve the underlying personality dynamics they protect (Fine 1982, Freud 1912a,b, Gabbard 1990). As Semrad admonished simply, "You don't go along with resistance" (Rako and Mazer 1983, p. 116).

As early psychoanalytic clinical theory became more sophisticated, resistance came to be viewed as a valuable source of information about the patient. Reich (1972) specifically focused on the resistances a patient manifested as a representation of underlying character development and pathology. Although his later activities brought censure, Reich's emphasis on resistance as information (and thus valuable) moved psychoanalytic clinical theory away from the view that resistances are merely oppositional phenomena to be conquered. Current psychodynamic clinical theory has generally accommodated itself to these dual views of resistance, that it is both opposition to the change(s) offered by psychotherapy and a source of developmental information about the patient (Gabbard 1990).

Traditional admonitions on the treatment of resistance reflect this conceptualization. Resistance is respected as important information about the patient, especially his characteristic defenses. However, it is also addressed via interpretation, with an ultimate goal of resolving (i.e., overcoming) it so that the repressed material protected by the resistance may be worked through. The process of interpretively working through resistances and the material shielded by them, in conjunction with similarly working through transference phenomena, constitutes the core of traditional psychodynamic technique (Gabbard 1990, Mendelsohn 1992). Schafer (1983) presents this well:

> . . . when the analysand is evidently and conflictedly avoiding or deferring change which, on the basis of explicit discussion, already makes analytic sense, that [is] a matter for the analyst to try to understand and then, if the time is ripe, to convey that understanding in a tactful, even if somewhat confronting interpretation. [pp. 167–168]

Schafer also warns that, "On the whole, however, the analyst must always be careful not to impose his or her value judgments on the analysand by unilaterally prescribing change" (p. 168).

Kohut (1977, 1984) challenged the conceptualization of resistance as working against the successful completion of treatment. Most notably in his last work, Kohut (1984) emphasized the adaptive functions of resistance. He proposed that the primary function of resistance is to protect the patient from narcissistic injuries either arising from lapses in the empathy of the psychotherapist or engendered by identity disruption. Change of any type, but certainly the fundamental changes that can result from psychotherapy, create identity disruptions. These disjunctive or fragmenting experiences are exquisitely painful.

Kohut questioned the utility and wisdom of attempting to overcome resistances. Instead, he suggested that the therapist use patient resistances as cues to understanding the interaction between ther-

apist and patient, especially as they could offer information about the therapist's level of empathic
immersion in the patient's experience. Resistances
suggest that the therapist is not responding empathically to the patient; either the therapist's actions are
touching old wounds without sensitivity or he or she
is missing cues that the patient is experiencing moments of fragmentation.

The notion that resistances serve a narcissistically protective function for the patient is important.
Rather than guarding repressed material which, if
worked through, could lead to change, resistance
serves to protect the patient from both the inevitable
lapses of therapist empathy inherent in the therapist's humanity and the narcissistic injuries inherent
in change.

Change is potentially narcissistically injurious to
the gay man in two distinct ways. First, change
threatens identity cohesion. As noted above, one of
the core difficulties presented by gay men involves an
alienation from the authentic nucleus of feelings,
fantasies, desires, and so on, that form the true self,
and the construction of a false self to achieve acceptance, approval, and affection. Resistances grow out
of the need to keep the false self, the only identity the
patient knows, vigorous. To discover that it is a
self-deceptive structure and that his internal life is an
unexplored realm is injurious indeed. Further, the
false self developed because of the patient's early
recognition that his authentic identity was not acceptable. For the gay man this probably involved his
innate sense of his homosexuality and the recognition of his immersion in a culture that overwhelming
rejects homosexuality. Resistances can regulate the

pace by which the patient discovers/creates his authentic core identity.

BARRY: RESISTANCE AS A MEANS OF SLOWING THERAPY'S PACE

Barry was a 28-year-old gay man who originally consulted me because of concerns that he did not know how to maintain a romantic relationship. After a series of sexual involvements that were initially exciting but quickly disappointing, he questioned his suitability for a relationship, even though he sincerely wanted one.

Over the first few weeks of his therapy Barry revealed that his greatest difficulty was not relationships with other men. This was actually a secondary difficulty to the relationship he maintained with himself. He described himself as perpetually lonely. When alone he felt guilty and "hyper"; it was extremely difficult for him to modulate his anxiety or soothe himself. He found it difficult to articulate his feelings and even more difficult to articulate desires or goals for his life.

In the first few months of his therapy Barry described a lonely and deprived childhood. Despite financial means, his parents were tightfisted with money. They were even more miserly with affection and affirmation for their child. He had cognitive memory of these deprivations but could not recall any feelings he had during childhood, nor could he empathically assign any feelings to himself as an adult remembering his childhood. His only approximations of feelings were "lonely" and "depressing," but these seemed to be less descriptors of authentic feeling states than words to describe an internal void.

In our work together, we began to reconstruct how it must have felt to be the boy in this environment. This led to memories of his earliest peer relationships. He always felt himself an outsider—the one who did not belong. He began to articulate this as an awareness of his homosexuality and a deep sense of shame that he was different from the other boys. "I couldn't understand why any of them would like me. I couldn't look their mothers in the eye when they were nice to me."

To the best of his memory, and with corroboration from external indices (e.g., school grades, conduct reports, awards, etc.), Barry was a "model child." He accommodated almost every request, even if it was to his detriment to do so. As an adult he had changed very little. Anyone's request became his command. There was a good deal of evidence that beneath his obliging acquiescence was resentment and rage.

As we began to get to know the man beneath the accommodating facade—a man of complex and contradictory emotions—Barry began to miss sessions. When he did come for an appointment, he was often several minutes late. I was bewildered. Our work had been going so well in my estimation. After all, we were achieving *my* goal of discovering Barry's true self. However, it began to dawn on me after three weeks into this deviated schedule that I was missing the point.

Barry arrived about ten minutes late for the fourth session into the sequence of missed and abbreviated appointments. Sitting down, he acknowledged the interruptions in our recent schedule. "I'm sorry," he offered, "I'm really not sure what's been happening lately—but I'm going to try to get back on track."

"Well," I responded, "I very much appreciate your consideration in apologizing—but I wonder if you're the one who owes an apology?"

"What do you mean?" he asked, clearly surprised.

"I mean I may owe you an apology," I responded. He looked quizzically at me and I continued, "I think I got lost in how much I *assumed* you were getting out of our work, that I missed you telling me that you were either getting too much out of it or not what *you* wanted most out of it. So, you found a way to tell me—a way that I couldn't miss."

Barry protested that therapy had been helpful to him and he valued our work together. However, he acknowledged that he had been feeling more anxious recently and also somewhat "confused and kind of hazy." He reported an appreciation of my apology. I retreated a little from my more active approach to Barry's therapy, determined to let things unfold at his pace. Our schedule returned to its previous regularity and Barry noted a decrease in his anxiety.

Throughout the remainder of his successful eighteen-month psychotherapy, there were minor moments of resistance, but none that threatened the continuity of our work—and each could be traced to an empathic lapse on my part. Had I not responded to this initial powerful resistance in the way that I did (i.e., responding to it as an assertion of the need to slow our pace) and proceeded to try interpretively to overcome it (i.e., responding to it as a defensive cover

for some repressed memory or affect, to be removed),
Barry would probably have ended his therapy at that
point.

RESISTANCE AS AN EXPRESSION OF THE
FEAR OF HOPE

The second potential narcissistic injury inherent in
change is the activation of hope, with the subsequent
opportunities for disappointment that this provides.
The gay man experiences a milieu of devaluation
ranging from covert disapproval to overt hatred
throughout most of his life. Without extraordinary
circumstances that provide affirmation and approval,
he develops a world view that includes his being
devalued as inherent. However, hope also seems to be
an irrevocable part of the human being's internal
construction.

After repeated instances of hoping, which lead to
disappointment, one learns to keep careful hold of the
propensity to hope. Gay men are generally particularly guarded in their willingness to hope (and often
staunchly determined not to hope). The possibility
that an environment might exist in which a gay man
is affirmed in his totality seems almost beyond the
realm of possibility. There are often relationships
(e.g., with lovers, friends, even parents) in which he
feels accepted and affirmed, but seldom are these
relationships perceived as strong enough to contain
the entirety of his internal experience. (In this way
gay men are little different from any other human
being; there are very few relationships in life that
offer the complete freedom for one to simply be, in all

one's rich complexities, short of competently pro-vided psychoanalysis or psychotherapy, which only imperfectly approximates this state.)

Involvement with an empathic psychotherapist gently arouses the patient's hope that it may be possible to be completely oneself with another person without injury to either oneself or the other person. This hope is frightening and leads to increased efforts to minimize the hope, and with it the potential for disappointment. Moments of resistance are often mo-ments of a focused and intense effort to minimize hope (Cornett 1993b).

JASON: RESISTANCE AS A MINIMIZATION OF HOPE

Jason was a 35-year-old man involved in a relation-ship of eleven years' duration. He began psycho-therapy because of "depression." Never in his life, he related, had he really experienced joy, but over the last two years his mood had become "darker than before." Nothing seemed to inspire happiness. His sleep schedule was irregular and he was persistently tired and irritable; he was also prone to outbursts of rage. He could not link his increased depression with any manifest changes in his life.

Over the first several weeks of our work, Jason detailed a traumatic developmental history. He grew up in a very small southeastern town. His parents were devout members of a fundamentalist Protestant church. This church taught that only certain types of people would be "saved" (i.e., allowed to enter Heaven after death). Some types would be absolutely barred from salvation; homosexuals were among this latter group. Jason described himself as an effeminate boy, taunted and teased by classmates throughout his school years. It was during elementary school that he had first been called "a homo," confirming what he instinctively knew about himself—even though he could not cognitively describe the meaning of the term. Such negative identity confirmation is common for young homosexual boys who do not conform to gender norms (Friedman 1988, Green 1987).

During his high school years Jason had been isolated and lonely. He did not enjoy sporting events, the only escape for the young people of the town. He read instead, which further alienated him from his peers. He believed himself to be the only homosexual person on the planet. In high school he dated girls to "prove to everybody, including me, that *it* wasn't true." However, with every unfulfilling heterosexual date his shame intensified.

After high school Jason met Michael, who became his lover. He was so appreciative of finding another homosexual man that he tried to overlook some obvious incompatibilities between them. Michael seemed to be as inexperienced as Jason and the couple had difficulties, especially in developing a satisfying sexual relationship. After about five years both began to seek sexual contacts outside the relationship. However, for Jason, these extrarelational contacts were guilt inducing and left him depleted. In the initial passion of an encounter with a new man, he could feel affirmation and something approximating appreciative acceptance. Even though he knew that this was not "real love," these moments gave him a taste of something he desperately hungered for as a constant in his life, but knew would always be out of reach. It was against this developmental context that Jason announced when he first consulted me that he was living in Hell now and knew that after he died that he would spend eternity in Hell.

As we worked together, Jason's affect gradually brightened, but he was constantly critical of himself, especially as he talked of hopes for the future. I began to offer observations that these criticisms seemed to follow expressions of hope—almost as counterweights. He accepted these observations thoughtfully. Gradually, he began to talk about his dissatisfaction with the relationship he maintained with Michael. He acknowledged that this relationship fit a pattern of disappointment in his life. Toward the end of one session he wistfully wondered aloud if he might someday experience a more satisfying love. He quickly dismissed this thought, but smiled as if the dismissal did not entirely rob him of the hope. The session ended on this note.

When Jason appeared for his next hour he was visibly distressed, saying he had become "more depressed than I ever have been before." He suggested that therapy might be harmful to him. He did not know who he was becoming, "but whoever he is, I don't like him; he's selfish and only interested in his own happiness." He informed me that if this was what psychotherapy was all about, then he probably wanted no more of it.

I offered responses that acknowledged how distressed he felt—and how guilty.

He snapped that when "you're becoming a selfish bastard you're supposed to feel guilty." "Look," he finally proposed, "you've got a pretty hopeless case here. I just whine about how horrible my life is and I'm sure that you have other people who could use the time better than I do." He seemed utterly dejected.

"You seem pretty down right now," I offered. He nodded wearily. "If you want to stop therapy, that's always your prerogative, but I guess I would question something you said."

"What's that?" he grumbled.

"The part about you being hopeless," I responded. "In fact, I would suggest that just the opposite is happening. You are, or rather were, feeling hope*ful* last time we met. Given your history and the end that was scripted for you so long ago—that Hell is inescapable for you both in this life and the next—it makes sense that hope is a dangerous commodity, to be avoided at all costs."

"What are you talking about?" he demanded, his facial expression conveying something of both rage and exquisite sadness.

"If you don't hope, you won't be disappointed. You have begun to break that cardinal rule and you don't recognize yourself as a man who can hope that there is more to his life than pain and sadness. You know the old saying 'Pride goeth before a fall'?" I asked, pulling up one of my family's hope preventatives.

"Yeah," Jason grunted.

"Maybe the philosophy that your family imposed upon you is 'Hope goeth before disappointment,'" I offered.

Jason cried. He spent much of the rest of that hour discussing his deep fear that allowing himself to hope too much would ensure devastating pain.

Jason's therapy was difficult. It lasted over three years and was characterized by much resistance to hoping and much mourning over the pain of his development. We had many such interchanges as the one described above. However, over time, the intensity of his dread of hope lessened and he ultimately ended our work, returning to graduate school and, while still living with Michael as a roommate, dating a man with whom he had much in common and with whom he felt very much in love.

I am not suggesting that resistance can be completely eliminated if the therapist is empathic enough. As Freud (1912b) proposed, resistance is ubiquitous to dynamically oriented psychotherapy. However, it is important how resistance is conceptualized. In neither of the cases above was resistance a hindrance to psychotherapy needing to be overcome. In both cases it served a protective function for the patient that warranted respect and acceptance. Understanding and accepting resistances, rather than attempting to conquer, undermine, or remove them, serves the psychotherapist and patient well in the long term. For the psychotherapist working with a gay man, approaching resistances in this manner may aid the patient in receiving all that is available from the treatment experience.

RECONCEPTUALIZING THE PRIMARY GOAL OF PSYCHOTHERAPY

Menaker (1989), echoing Rank, admonishes that psychotherapy is never value-free. She quotes his caution that "Whether it has to do with the medical concept of normality or with the social concept of adaptation, therapy can never be without prejudice, for it sets out from the standpoint that something should be otherwise than it is, no matter how one may formulate it" (p. 42). Throughout the remainder of this text the activities of the psychotherapist in his or her work with the gay man are described. However, these activities are directed toward a goal other than change in the patient. The function of psychotherapy technique is to create an environment in which the patient is able to explore his identity if he so chooses. The goal is not the outcome (the patient may or may not change aspects of himself); the goal for the psychotherapist is to function as a reliable selfobject and, in the process, create an environment that affirms the patient, whether he changes or does not. Thus, change in the patient's life, if it occurs at all, is potentially a positive outcome of the treatment (although often one of some ambivalence for the patient), but is a byproduct and not the sought result. All of that said, I return to Rank's admonition and acknowledge that it would be naive to propose that the belief that one have a solid, cohesive identity is not a value that to some extent will influence the activities of the psychotherapist. By taking the approach that will be described in the chapters that follow, however, I believe that the influence of this value can be kept in a perspective that does not simply make the patient an automaton, attempting to live up to the therapist's expectations.

If the therapist is successful in creating an empathic and affirming environment, there is likely to be some positive change in the patient's life. Based on this, one could reasonably ask why it is important to avoid conceptualizing change as the endeavor's goal. Some important reasons were outlined earlier in the chapter. These include the interference of the therapist's value system in the treatment and the potential result(s) of this interference on the patient's freedom to discover/create his own identity. However, there are three additional reasons to emphasize this point.

First, defining the primary goal of psychotherapy as the process of treatment rather than the outcome offers the therapist a goal over which he or she has some real control. Too many skilled and well-intentioned psychotherapists become narcissistically injured if treatment with a given patient does not achieve what they would consider to be a desirable result. A goal of inducing change in another person, something over which we have no real control, leaves one narcissistically vulnerable. Sometimes, to alleviate this vulnerability or soothe a resultant injury, the therapist unwittingly pursues change at an ultimate cost to the patient.

The second reason to avoid considering change the primary goal of psychotherapy is intimately related to the first. The therapist must avoid involvement in the maintenance of a primary (i.e., developmental) false self, or iatrogenic creation of a variant false self. As the false self is the product of expectations for compliance, the patient is likely to oblige if faced with the therapist's expectations for change. Paradoxically, change ceases to be change under such circumstances and becomes an expression of the status quo. Instead of helping the patient break the shackles of trading authenticity for acceptance, the therapist actually strengthens those shackles.

Finally, it is important for the therapist to remember that gay men are an oppressed group in our culture. They can easily assume the identity of victimhood. A staunch focus on change communicates that the patient is flawed (which is often attributed by the patient to his homosexuality) and that he must become different to achieve wholeness. This view can encourage the patient to see himself as inherently inferior and thus the victim of the larger heterosexual culture. Such a perception militates against the assumption of personal responsibility. One of the accurate complaints that social critics (e.g., Lasch 1979) have lodged against psychotherapy is that it can rob patients of their right/obligation to personal responsibility. The view that change is a paramount goal to the therapeutic endeavor has been a paradoxical and subtle bulwark of this phenomenon.

SUMMARY

Every paradigm of psychotherapy maintains a philosophy regarding the goal of the endeavor and the most efficacious means of reaching that goal. A traditional—and, on the surface, logical—goal has been to aid the patient in changing internally in a way that brings relief from his distress. The means of achieving this goal has generally involved diagnosis followed by treatment of the syndrome or disorder identified through the diagnostic process.

This chapter has identified several difficulties with this philosophical perspective generally and in its application to gay men specifically. Chief among these difficulties is the potential to undercut the patient's search for his authentic self as he accommodates his identity to the health values of the psycho-therapist that are manifested in the diagnosis that therapy is focused on ameliorating.

A much more helpful perspective on the goal of psychotherapy is to view it as a process of creating an environment that facilitates understanding the pa-tient as he searches out his authentic self. Change may indeed result from this process—happily in-cluding symptomatological relief—however, change must be seen as a byproduct of psychotherapy, not its goal, in order to truly offer the patient as accepting an environment as possible in the event that he chooses to search out and accept his authentic self.

With a perspective on what psychotherapy can truly hope to offer a gay man outlined, it is now possible to elaborate on the skills that the psychother-apist can employ to create an environment and expe-rience that offers the patient the opportunity to discover/create his authentic identity.

II

CLINICAL
ISSUES

4

Anonymity and Neutrality in the Relational Environment

Existentialist psychotherapy prefers . . . the use of another interpersonal experience, "encounter." Encounter is, in general, not so much the fortuitous meeting and first acquaintance of two individuals, but rather the decisive inner experience resulting from it for one (sometimes for both) of the two individuals. Something totally new is revealed, new horizons open, one's *weltanschauung* is revised, and sometimes the whole personality is restructured.

Henri F. Ellenberger

RECONCEPTUALIZING A TRADITIONAL CONTEXT

In achieving the primary goal of psychotherapy proposed in the previous chapter—offering an environment that affirms the patient and invites the possibility of discovering/creating his true self—the context in which the treatment takes place is an important factor. This context, with all its human dimensions, creates an ambiance that either facilitates or hinders the therapeutic work. Psychodynamic clinical theory has long recognized this fact. Two of the most important constructs offered by psychodynamic theory concerning the human environment of psychotherapy are anonymity and neutrality. However, as these constructs have traditionally been conceived, they are not of optimal aid to the gay man. This chapter focuses on reconceptualizing these two aspects of the therapeutic environment to ensure that this environment is of maximum benefit to the gay patient.

THERAPIST ANONYMITY

Freud (1913, 1940) emphasized the importance of maintaining a therapeutic setting that guarded the anonymity of the analyst. The environment he prescribed for his disciples was an austere one, almost antiseptic: "The Doctor should be opaque to his patients and, like a mirror, should show them nothing but what is shown to him" (Freud 1912b, p. 118). He even suggested that the analyst's physical appearance could disrupt the work of analysis. For that reason, Otto Rank, who apparently concurred with Freud's assessment that he was homely, sat in a darkened corner of his consulting room while working with patients (Lieberman 1985, Menaker 1989). Langs and Stone (1980) describe an analyst who sat behind a screen while working with patients to avoid her countenance contaminating their projections. Both Langs and Stone criticize such a position as being that of a caricature, but it, as well as Rank's position, are logical extremes of an emphasis on anonymity. Although most analysts and psychotherapists do not approach this level of concern with anonymity, a fairly austere environment has been generally accepted as a basic tenet of psychoanalysis and psychodynamic psychotherapy.

Interestingly, the environment that Freud provided for his patients was hardly anonymous. His antiquities collections were an integral part of his consulting room and his pet chow often sat in on sessions. Photographs of himself, friends, and family decorated the walls. He shared a meal with the Rat Man and, although he warned against analysts treating people with whom they had interactions outside of therapy, he did not abide by this admonition. He, indeed, analyzed his own daughter, Anna. In short, the environment Freud offered his patients was singularly his. His tastes, preferences, interests, and passions—in short his identity—were indelibly and unmistakably imprinted on that environment (Gay 1988).

Those early analysts who followed Freud struggled with anonymity and its maintenance, with greater and lesser degrees of success. Many, like Ferenczi, Rank, and Adler, disagreed with Freud on basic theoretical concepts, among them the need for therapist anonymity. For their theoretical heresies these men were expelled from the psychoanalytic inner sanctum. The level of anonymity that the analyst was willing to maintain, among other things, became a measure of whether he or she practiced orthodox psychoanalysis or "wild analysis" (Freud 1910).

There was little innovation in thinking about the environment of psychoanalysis and psychotherapy—especially regarding anonymity—by orthodox psychoanalysts for many years after Freud's death. Ferenczi and Rank offered much original and creative thinking in this regard, but had left the fold of orthodoxy, which made their ideas anathema to the mainstream (Lieberman 1985, Stanton 1991). Alexander (1963, Alexander, French, et al. 1974), too, in his explications of the "corrective emotional experience" challenged some basic assumptions of psychoanalytic technique. However, even though he emphasized the therapist assuming complementary roles to the patient's transference, he did not significantly challenge the role of therapist anonymity in the process of psychoanalysis and psychotherapy.

The next period of real interest in the environment of psychotherapy began with Winnicott, who compared the helpful psychotherapeutic environment to the environment provided by a "good enough mother" (Winnicott 1965). He referred to a therapeutic environment provided by a good enough therapist as a holding or facilitating environment. The holding environment symbolically re-created the safety and serenity of the mother's measured permissiveness and restraint.

> The mother holds the situation, and does so over and over again, and at a critical period in the baby's life. The consequence is that something can be done about something. The mother's technique enables the in-

fant's co-existing love and hate to become sorted out and interrelated and gradually brought under control from within in a way that is healthy. [quoted by Khan in Winnicott 1986, p. 16]

Winnicott, like Freud, could also apparently be quite authentic and warm with patients, even touching them and revealing personal aspects of himself (Little 1990).

Langs (1976, 1982) has perhaps been the most prolific contemporary theorist on the role of the environment in psychotherapy. Building on Winnicott's idea of the holding environment, Langs (Langs and Stone 1980) has proposed that a set of basic and inviolable rules for psychotherapy form a frame for the treatment that functions in the same way that a picture frame forms a boundary around the artwork it borders.

. . . think of the frame of a painting as setting off the reality inside from the reality outside. So the frame does two things: it demands a sphere of influence—in other words, it creates a boundary. And it also indicates that within the frame, the laws of interaction and communication can be different from those that prevail outside. [p. 45]

Langs (1982) asserts that the rules of the frame include strict privacy and confidentiality, relative therapist anonymity, therapist neutrality, and a set schedule with set fees. Over the years he has modified his views of the constitution of the frame. For instance, in an early book on technique (Langs 1973), he asserts that a therapist's office located in his or her home presents challenges, although not insurmountable ones, to the maintenance of the frame. However, in a later text (Langs 1982) he concludes that home office arrangements inherently compromise the integrity of the frame, in large measure because they compromise the anonymity of the therapist.

Langs (1982) differentiates "relative anonymity" from austerity. He argues for a measure of comfort in the surroundings that the patient will inhabit, but also argues that such surroundings must be ambiguous and avoid revealing too much of the therapist. While acknowledging that some revelations of the therapist's personality and character are unavoidable in his or her style of dress, taste in furniture, and so on, he stresses the need to avoid revelations beyond the absolute, inherent minimum.

Langs has been roundly criticized for the rigid dogma of his views. Stone (Langs and Stone 1980) is representative of this criticism when he admonishes that "it is important to remember (if, indeed, it is recognized at all!) that passive adherence to rules can also take on a negative twist with certain patients, at certain junctures" (p. 47). However, Langs' thinking about anonymity does not seem inconsistent with the larger psychoanalytic community. Moore and Fine (1990a), for instance, define anonymity as "the state of being unknown. In psychoanalysis, personal facts about the analyst should remain unknown to the analysand" (p. 23). While they also acknowledge that there are revelations inherent in basic demographic facts about the analyst, and that with patients manifesting severe psychopathology some personal revelation may be unavoidable, they propose that such revelations "usually [impede] psychoanalytic progress by limiting the breadth of transference projections and their availability for interpretation" (p. 23).

As Stone notes, rigid adherence to rules sometimes offers no real benefit to patients. I would add that rigid adherence to rules, including anonymity, can indeed, at times be destructive. Early admonitions regarding the setting of psychoanalysis and psychotherapy, especially those relating to anonymity, have held sway in the psychodynamic community for over sixty years. However, these admonitions, which Freud did not observe (suggesting that they were not as inviolable in the care of patients as he suggested), were developed for a specific type of patient. Many groups of patients—including male homosexuals—were largely excluded from treatment. And, as May (1953) proposes, it is important to remember that the early adherents of psychoanalysis practiced and formulated their views of treatment before what he terms "the age of emptiness."

In working with gay men the psychotherapist is well advised to maintain a flexible attitude toward the treatment frame, including relative anonymity. It is necessary to offer an environment characterized by boundaries. The patient may come to define himself via these boundaries and in juxtaposition to the therapist within them. However, an austere and anonymous environment is generally not helpful. The authentic therapist should be available within the environment in which he or she practices. An antiseptic environment, peopled by an anonymous (or, at the extreme, only minimally existent) therapist does not demonstrate the courage of authenticity, nor does it invite the patient to muster the courage to be authentic.

Another conception of the therapist's role in the treatment process was offered by Sullivan (1954). He proposed that the therapist functions as a *participant-observer*. The therapist is an observer of the patient's world, attempting to understand that world. To do that the therapist must ensure, to the extent possible, that his or her personality does not overwhelm the patient. However, the therapist is also involved as a participant in the drama of the patient's world and must therefore be emotionally involved as an authentic self.

THE PSYCHOTHERAPIST AS SELFOBJECT

For the gay man who is struggling with the search for acceptance and affirmation, the therapist must be genuinely available to serve as an empathic selfobject. Boundaries are crucial and the therapist must not place the patient's needs in a subordinate role to his or her own needs, which requires constant and conscientious attention to the motivations for personal revelations. But the multidimensional process of acquiring and communicating empathy requires the engagement of the therapist on such a basic emotional and intellectual level that anonymity is precluded.

Attempting to maintain the posture of anonymity can significantly interfere in the therapist's ability to function as a reliable selfobject. This is especially true if the patient's search for his true self involves development in the twinship and idealizing spheres of the self. If the psychotherapist is a gay man, the dilemma is all the more acute.

The gay male psychotherapist can function reliably as a mirroring selfobject while striving to be relatively anonymous more effectively than he can in the other two spheres because mirroring selfobject responses are focused almost exclusively on acknowledging and appreciating the patient's accomplishments, competent functioning, and moments of pride. There is a need for authenticity in the sense that the therapist must be able to truly accept and reflect moments of assertion and pride, something that our culture has great difficulty in doing with gay men and something that may be equally difficult for early caregivers due to either the patient's homosexuality or their own narcissistic difficulties. Feigning such acceptance negates true empathy and results in a saccharine appeasement that is ultimately condescending, the opposite of empathy. However, the need for authenticity is different in the development of the idealizing and twinship spheres of the self.

Because gay men have so few developmental opportunities to idealize and merge with accepting figures, it is important that they be able to achieve this with the psychotherapist, especially if that therapist is a gay man. The patient is often hungry to idealize a man—something he has perhaps found impossible prior to engagement with the therapist due to the reluctance of caregivers to tolerate this. He is also often hungry for the experience of being confirmed as a man among men and, more importantly, as a gay man among gay men (i.e., the yearning for twinship experiences). Since the gay man is often deprived of the early twinship selfobject experiences that confirm identity (i.e., not only with his father, but also through the peer relationships that Sullivan [1953] referred to as "chum" relationships), this is an area often focused upon with the therapist. These twinship selfobject experiences transpire for the child in the verbal and nonverbal give and take among the youngster, parents, and peers. The same confirmation process also takes place in regard to ethnicity, culture, and sexual orientation. However, the homosexual boy is deprived of many, if not most, of these opportunities.

In psychotherapy the gay man often hungers for twinship selfobject experiences. Many of these experiences take place through his comparison of himself to the gay male therapist and through the myriad subtle interactions that confirm the pair as similar. As is the case with most patients, he hungers to know the true essence of the therapist's character and personality (Glover 1937, Langs and Stone 1980).

Much of who the therapist is becomes evident through his interactions with the patient. So I am not suggesting that psychotherapy become a sort of "show and tell." Indeed, one's true character shows through to patients no matter what one reveals or fails to reveal. The argument is not for constant or continual revelation on the part of the therapist. This would meet only the therapist's needs and would overwhelm the patient. However, because gay men have so few developmental opportunities in our society to feel a part of a larger community, it is often important that the gay male therapist who wishes to function as an empathic twinship selfobject be willing to reveal and/or confirm aspects of his identity (Cornett 1990).

THE RELATIONSHIP BETWEEN THERAPIST ANONYMITY AND SHAME

Isay (1993b) proposes two other inherent difficulties with therapist anonymity when both the therapist and patient are gay men. First, Isay notes that the failure of a homosexual psychotherapist or psychoanalyst to acknowledge his homosexuality, especially when questioned directly by a patient, may be done primarily out of shame, rather than the protection of anonymity. The refusal to acknowledge one's homosexuality communicates hatred and loathing for one's identity. Patients can hardly be expected not to internalize this aspect of the therapist as they internalize the empathic and otherwise helpful aspects of the therapist and the therapeutic relationship. The psychotherapist's refusal to acknowledge his homosexuality can hardly invite the patient to embrace his. Indeed, the therapist's shame regarding his homosexuality invites the patient to feel ashamed of his homosexuality.

The second difficulty that Isay notes with the therapist's refusal to acknowledge his homosexuality under the guise of maintaining anonymity is a variation of the first. It involves the patient's assumption, based on shame, that the therapist must be heterosexual.

The heterosexual assumption is most commonly made by heterosexual patients. But it is also made by many gay men and lesbians who internalize society's prejudice (Isay 1989), leading some to believe that they are defective or sick and therefore that anyone from whom they are seeking assistance must be heterosexual. [Isay 1993b, p.181]

Isay argues that the homosexual therapist's disclosure of his sexual orientation provides the patient with a model of integrity, authenticity, and pride that subtly challenges the patient's self-hatred. He also observes that it does so without hindering transference elaboration (see also Nash 1993). This self-disclosure need not disrupt the psychotherapist's typical curiosity regarding the motivations of the patient's questioning his sexual orientation, the patient's fantasies in this regard, or the patient's response to his self-revelation.

A NOTE CONCERNING RESEARCH REGARDING THERAPIST SELF-DISCLOSURE

Because therapist self-disclosure has been such a controversial area in psychotherapy, it has been the focus of much anecdotal and quantitative research (Chesner and Baumeister 1985, Cozby 1973). On the whole, these studies have failed to support the notion that *reasonable* therapist self-disclosures (i.e., disclosures neither extensive enough nor so intimately personal that they overwhelm the patient) that are the result of an empathic focus on the patient are inherently deleterious to psychotherapy, as some clinicians conclude (Chernus 1992, Langs 1982). Further, both the anecdotal and quantitative research suggest that the majority of psychodynamically oriented psychotherapists self-disclose at times and believe that to do so is to some extent helpful (Anderson and Mandell 1989, Cornett 1990, Hill et al. 1988, Palombo 1987, Ramsdell and Ramsdell 1994, Searles 1990).

Studies have also focused on variables found to be helpful from the perspective of patients. These studies confirm that therapist self-disclosure is among the most helpful of therapist interventions. For instance, Hill and colleagues (1988) discovered that of nine therapist response modes measured (including approval, information, direct guidance, paraphrase, interpretation, and confrontation), patients believed therapist self-disclosure to be the most helpful. Ramsdell and Ramsdell (1993) note, in a similar study, "even years after the termination of treatment, clients tend to regard counselor self-disclosure as beneficial to their therapy" (p. 211). When questioned, the subjects in Hill and colleagues' study emphasized that self-disclosure lessened the power differential they felt between themselves and their therapists and also emphasized the human connection shared by the two parties. This seems to be an important description of the twinship selfobject function(s) that therapist self-disclosure can serve.

ALLEN: A TWINSHIP SELFOBJECT EXPERIENCE

Allen was a 27-year-old gay man seen in twice weekly psychotherapy. He originally sought psychotherapy because of a strong desire to be involved in a romantic relationship and his seeming inability to do so. Allen was both quite handsome and sexually seductive. He related that he often found willing sexual partners and he could engage them in short-lived relationships, but he could not retain their interest for longer than a few weeks. Frustrated and hurt, he decided that there must be something he was "doing wrong."

Allen was reared in a family with one sibling and, as we discovered over the course of his therapy, two very narcissistically impaired parents. It became clear to Allen very early in his life that his primary function in the family was to meet his parents' needs. He routinely accomplished tasks that were within the parental realm and that required the skills of an adult to be achieved without considerable anxiety and frustration. Allen often "covered" for his parents who were both alcoholic. From the age of 6 on he often organized and/or carried out activities to ensure that his parents did not lose their respective jobs due to the alcoholism. These activities included enlisting neighbors to call in "sick" for the parents, arranging alternate transportation to school for him and his brother, and so on.

Allen had few friends as a child. Like many children in alcoholic homes, he was afraid to bring other children home from school because he was never sure what parental state of intoxication would greet him and his guests. He was also required to babysit for his younger brother, even when his parents were home, so that they could be free to drink without interruption; thus, he had few opportunities to go to classmates' homes.

During his psychotherapy, Allen related that he

had known he was homosexual from the age of 8. He remembered very intense crushes on boys when he was in the third grade. However, he also knew that homosexuality was "morally wrong." At about age 6, he had heard his parents discussing some "funny" men in the city in which the family lived. At 8 or 9 he remembered them fairly seething with contempt as they explained to him, both drunk, that he must stay away from "men who like boys" (he remembered knowing that this referred to all homosexuals, not simply pedophiles). They informed him that all "homos" would anally rape him (which they described in severely anxiety-provoking detail) and then leave him with a disease (as this was before the advent of the AIDS pandemic, they were presumably referring to other sexually transmitted diseases). Allen was deeply ashamed of his homosexuality because the guiding principle of his life was to avoid parental disappointment. His homosexuality was suppressed altogether until he was 22 and then for two years he minimized the importance of his homo-erotic masturbatory fantasies and even homosexual encounters as meaning nothing about his sexual orientation, which he maintained was heterosexual.

It became apparent very early in Allen's therapy that he had no fundamental sense of himself. For the first several months he tried with much intensity to assess my reaction to everything he said, acknowledging that he wished not to offend or disappoint me. He attempted to defer decisions to me and wanted all matters to be convenient for me. I gently and appreciatively, but firmly, refused to make decisions that were legitimately his. In this atmosphere he gradually became sad and anxious.

However, along with Allen's deepening sadness came a curiosity about himself. Regarding our work together, he would need to make decisions because I was unwilling to. He therefore needed to know how he felt about the options available to him. Gradually, as his sense of himself grew and became more secure, he also developed a genuine curiosity about me (i.e., one not focused solely on my approval or disapproval of him). This was a curiosity founded on a desire to compare himself to me and, in this process, differentiate himself further.

Allen knew me to be gay and that I had a lover and he became very curious about this relationship. (Another factor that often precludes anonymity for gay psychotherapists is the fact that in most areas, the gay community is much smaller than the larger heterosexual community and non-closeted gay men are more visible.) At this point it also gradually became apparent that in addition to his not having a deep and clear sense of himself to offer to another man, Allen's shame about being homosexual dramatically interfered in his search for a mate.

During one session Allen was talking about the inherent difficulty of integrating sexual desire into intimate romantic relationships and I wondered aloud if it was inherent in *all* romantic relationships that sex and intimacy be difficult to integrate (I quietly wondered to myself if splitting was involved in his dilemma). He became confused and I tried to clarify by stating that it seemed possible to integrate these two aspects of a relationship. He laughed and replied "That seems funny coming from you."

"Oh," I responded curiously, "what do you mean?"

Allen continued, "Because I understand that you keep those two a little separate."

"I do?" I posed.

"That's what I hear," he answered with a smile.

"I'm curious about what that means," I prodded.

"Well," he began somewhat mischievously, "I'm told that when you or your lover go out of town, you're free to sleep with other people—and you do."

"Huh . . . " I offered with a pause. "You heard that?"

For the first time in this interaction, Allen looked anxious and he acknowledged, "Yeah, some guys who know you told me."

"Well, what do you think about that—I mean that I have this sexual arrangement with my lover?" I asked.

"Of course, it's your business, but it seems to me that it means you don't *really* think sex and relationships are all that inseparable," he concluded.

There were a number of directions I could have pursued at that point in the discussion, but the pivotal issue seemed to be the one that had been present for some time; his curiosity about me and my world (i.e., a manifestation of twinship selfobject yearning). Because of its potentially shocking nature, Allen seemed to believe that he had authentic information, but he had presented it to me in a quizzical way. I decided to respond genuinely to his curiosity, as a twinship selfobject.

"Well," I began, "I think it's a natural part of therapy for you to be curious about me. It's also a way to figure out how we're alike and how we're different. I appreciate your sharing what you heard with me and I think it's always important for us to explore what you're thinking about me or our relationship. In terms of what you heard about my relationship, I'd like to offer a clarification about that, because the comparisons you make between us are best served by knowing what's genuinely me."

Allen looked curious.

I continued, "My lover and I have a very monogamous relationship—not because that's the only way to have a relationship and certainly not for moral reasons—but because our relationship reflects who we are. Other people may wish to have other kinds of relationships that reflect who they are. For us, monogamy is important." I responded to Allen's fantasy of my relationship, prompted or not by interference from parties external to his therapy, because it does seem that patients are best served by authentic knowledge of a person who develops an intimate and important place in their lives. They do compare themselves to therapists and do seek to use them as twinship selfobjects. Neither silence, interpretation, nor rebuff fulfills this very legitimate need. Beyond that, however, there was another reason for addressing this situation as I did. Allen and I are both gay men. He asked me something about myself as a gay man. It was something about my relationship, something of which I am very proud. It seemed that Allen's therapy would benefit more from my acknowledging, first, my pride in my identity as a gay man (Isay 1993b); second, my pride in my relationship; and finally, the fact that my relationship suited my lover and me—it reflected a solid sense of identity. Although no other gay couple has to share our value in this way, the value is authentic to us.

Allen mulled over this revelation for several weeks. Over the course of his therapy he concluded that he and I might indeed hold very different values on this issue. I affirmed this difference as a sign of his identity as a gay man separate from me, deserving of respect for his authentic identity and values. His curiosity remained for several months and there were a few further self-disclosures on my part. After two years Allen discontinued therapy, by all evidence pleased with the outcome. He had a lover—an affirming and creative man who supported Allen as he strove to exist separately from, but intimately involved in, the relationship. They were still negotiating the terms of their relationship and it was still evolving as Allen's therapy ended. Most importantly, however, Allen and his lover had developed a reciprocal relationship that afforded respect to both members of the couple as distinct, with different identities.

As we terminated, Allen returned to the moments of my self-disclosure as important to his discovery that everyone was not like his parents and that he could make decisions and hold different, even opposing, views of issues without someone being destroyed. He articulated a belief that he had discovered himself, in part, not only because of what I had not done (i.e., infantilize and narcissistically use him by making decisions for him, and so on) but also because of what I had done, especially offering him an interaction with someone striving to be authentic while not demanding that everyone had to be just like me.

THERAPIST NEUTRALITY

Therapist neutrality is another aspect of the therapeutic environment that finds disagreement among clinicians. Many contemporary psychoanalytic theorists consider neutrality and abstinence a single clinical concept (Moore and Fine 1990d). Others combine neutrality and anonymity (e.g., Mendelsohn 1992). For this discussion, neutrality will be considered a philosophical stance assumed by the psychotherapist in the therapeutic relationship. Abstinence will be considered an aspect of the emotional stance the psychotherapist maintains with the patient and will be explored in the next chapter as a part of countertransference. This differentiation is acknowledged to be one of personal preference, with arguments available to all for different configurations (Moore and Fine 1990d).

For many analytically oriented clinicians, neutrality concerns the clinician's stance vis-à-vis the structural hierarchy of the patient's internal world. In this conception, neutrality is the avoidance of prejudice toward any intrapsychic agency as inherently better than another; it is also considered a refusal to side with any particular structure over another involved in an internal conflict (Hoffer 1985). Schafer (1983) proposes that "in his or her neutrality, the analyst does not crusade for or against the so-called id, superego, or defensive ego. The analyst has no favorites and so is not judgmental" (p. 5).

Of interest in regard to neutrality conceived of in this way is the violation of it by many analytic clinicians in the psychoanalytic and psychotherapeutic treatment of homosexual men. Isay (1993a) catalogs a list of assaults on neutrality toward gay men in the psychodynamic literature. Socarides (1978) represents a blatant example of a disregard for neutrality in his assertion that

even the most serious cases of homosexuality will
yield to therapy if the patient seeks therapy when he
feels severely distressed about being homosexual, not
only because of guilt or shame but because he finds
his homosexual life meaningless and alien to the
biological realities of life around him. [p. 418]

He describes psychotherapeutic experiences involving an analyst demonstrating to a patient "by
diagrams of the external female genital system [that]
there was nothing to fear and that he certainly could
have heterosexual intercourse" (p. 210). He also rec-
ommends that the clinician "make an early interpretation that the patient's lack of sexual interest in
women is not due to the absence of heterosexual
desires but to his fear of women, which militates
against desire" (pp. 419–420).

Nicolosi (1993), in the conduct of so-called reparative therapy, a purportedly psychodynamically
based sexual reorientation "therapy" for gay men,
states in the presentation of a case:

At last, Tom [the patient] was committing himself
completely to overcoming his male attractions. I knew
it was a solution the Gay Rights Movement would
disdain. They would say it was dishonesty with one's
true self, hypocrisy—that sort of rhetoric. I had great
respect for Tom James; he had chosen the tough road,
yet *I believe it was the right one.* [p. 34, emphasis
added]

He notes further in a discussion of this case, which
involved a homosexual man who was heterosexually
married, that "I was not just a neutral therapist. I was

for the marriage and the diminishment of Tom's homosexuality" (p. 36). Neither Nicolosi nor Socarides demonstrates neutrality of any type in their discussions of clinical work with gay men.

Neutrality, however, is as essential an ingredient to the environment of psychotherapy for the homosexual man as it is for any other patient. Isay (1989, 1993a) has worked extensively with gay men seen previously by psychoanalysts and psychotherapists intent on effecting a change from homosexuality to heterosexuality. He concludes that neutrality is often an aspect of the therapeutic environment that is not afforded respect when the goal of treatment is sexual reorientation.

Another common difficulty of neutrality is that it is often equated with silence. From this perspective, the psychotherapist offers the patient a space in which to explore his internal world with minimal participation of the therapist. The philosophy of this type of neutrality seems to be the same as that of the old English common-law maxim *Qui tacet consentire* ("silence gives consent"). However, silence is often not interpreted as acceptance; instead it often seems to the patient, especially one accustomed to rejection, a type of cold judgment. Menaker (1989) discusses her analysis with Anna Freud and one particular session in which she had shared her indignation at the treatment of Jews in Vienna:

> It would have been helpful had Anna Freud shared in the conflict, shared in the indignation about prejudice and discrimination. . . . Instead I felt her silence as a judgment, for silence is never experienced as neutrality. Thus I learned from my own frustration not to

keep silent in response to my patients' strong and conflicting emotions. To echo similar or related feelings is a form of empathic understanding and helps us feel less alone, less guilty, and therefore less unworthy. [p. 51]

Isay proposes another conception of neutrality that is helpful in clinical work with gay men. He proposes neutrality to be a state of nonjudgmental curiosity. The analyst or therapist maintains an interest in and curiosity about the patient's internal life. Only in such a stance can the patient truly be discovered by himself and the clinician. Obviously, such a stance decries a priori assumptions regarding what and who the patient *should* be. Neutrality in this sense also encourages a sense of humility in the therapist that is appropriate to the endeavor of psychotherapy (Solomon 1992b).

By assuming such a neutral stance, the therapist invites the patient to view his life with curiosity. True curiosity both leads to real understanding and militates against condemnation. As curiosity and condemnation are mutually exclusive, the patient who is truly curious about himself is likely to reject condemnation as a way of treating himself.

Offering a homosexual patient an invitation to treat himself with understanding is important because condemnation of the self, encouraged by societal forces, is so omnipresent. In addition to doing so by assuming a neutral stance, the psychotherapist can offer this invitation through efforts to bring to the patient's awareness moments when he is treating himself contemptuously or dismissively. At the initiation of such efforts there is usually a look of bewilderment on the patient's face and he often argues for the validity of his view of himself (and even that he is being overly kind in his assessment of himself as "worthless," etc.). However, if the psychotherapist maintains a consistently accepting and curious stance while offering these observations, he invites the patient to learn to differentiate curiosity from contempt and generally awakens the patient's dormant curiosity about himself.

The reawakening of curiosity signals an interest in the discovery of the true self. It is a sign that the patient is beginning to evaluate the applicability of familial and social assessments of him. Such an evaluation may ultimately result in the patient's rejection of these assessments as customary ways of viewing the self. In short, the capacity of the psychotherapist to maintain a neutral stance in working with the patient will largely determine how free he is to discover/create his true self.

MITCH: CREATING NEUTRALITY
IN A SECOND PSYCHOTHERAPY EXPERIENCE

Mitch was a 34-year-old gay man who consulted me for psychotherapy after having been in treatment for approximately one year with a heterosexual psychotherapist who worked extensively with gay men. He announced during our first hour that he was "codependent" and wished to overcome this. He related that he had been in weekly psychotherapy with his previous therapist (who counted among her specialties the treatment of "codependence"), attended Codependents Anonymous meetings twice weekly, attended weekend workshops on codependence regularly, and read extensively books and articles suggested by his therapist.

Mitch spoke of his previous therapist with respect, although not a good deal of warmth. I found myself wondering why, after embarking on such an intensive treatment program with a therapist who specialized in what he said most troubled him, had Mitch consulted me. I asked him.

"I didn't get it with her," he began. "I thought maybe it was because she was straight—you know, maybe we spoke different languages." He suddenly appeared dejected. "I'm afraid, though, it's because I'm too screwed up."

I noted this harsh characterization internally and asked, "When you call yourself 'codependent' what do you mean?"

Mitch proceeded to articulate a list of what he termed "character flaws," including "wanting to control everyone," finding himself perpetually angry "with no reason," and "incapable of having a healthy relationship."

As the first hour ended I told Mitch that I would be happy to work with him, but I cautioned that "codependence" was not something I knew a great deal about. He appeared surprised and asked what my focus was. I responded that I try, as far as I am able, to deal with people and not syndromes; I would try to understand his world—including who he was, in all his complexity. Still looking a little perplexed, he agreed to give this "understanding stuff" a try.

Over the course of the first few hours with me Mitch detailed a relationship with a lover, Michael, that was unsatisfactory to him in many ways. He often felt devalued and discounted by this man who had been his lover for four years. They fought often and bitterly, exchanging exquisitely painful insults with each other. As he spoke of this relationship, Mitch often pejoratively labeled his own feelings, and wishes as "sick." I gradually began to call his attention to this process by gently challenging his "assessments" of himself as attacks. I likened his use of terms like *codependent, unhealthy, controlling*, and *sick* to calling himself names. Name-calling, while certainly his prerogative, blocked our, but especially his, developing a full understanding of all that he was. He seemed continually surprised that I would not join him in assaulting himself.

Early in the third month of his therapy Mitch was recounting a conflict between him and Michael, that seemed to center around Michael's refusal to acknowledge his feelings on a contested topic. He suddenly stopped and demanded: "Well, wasn't I being controlling—aren't you going to confront me about that?"

"It hadn't occurred to me to confront you," I offered, "because it hadn't occurred to me that you were being controlling."

"What?" he stammered incredulously.

"I may have missed something, but it seems to me that you were talking about a fight with Michael and that you were hurt and angry and wanted Michael to understand that," I responded.

Mitch asserted that Jan, his previous therapist, would use such fights to illustrate his "codependence" and point out the "unrealistic" and "controlling" aspects of his hunger for Michael's acknowledgment of his feelings. She would also, at

these junctures, offer alternative behavioral strategies for dealing with Michael.

Attempting to avoid an active role in splitting, I
responded: "Jan and I may think about therapy
differently—which to me is okay because there
doesn't seem to be any one absolutely right way to do
therapy—but I see understanding who you are and
what you want as more important than changing how
you do things. My experience is that when the first
happens, the second takes care of itself."

Throughout the first six months of his therapy
Mitch and I had many similar interchanges. Gradually, his descriptions of himself became less pseudo-
diagnostic and punitive. He began to explore a very
painful childhood. Over the next year he began to see
his adult functioning as understandable in light of his
childhood's many traumata. As he did so, he also
attempted new interpersonal strategies. A serendipi-
tous development also occurred in that Michael, perhaps under the pressure of a changing interpersonal
system, also changed many of his behavioral patterns. Harmony and satisfaction in the relationship
improved significantly. Most of Mitch's "codependent" traits that had so troubled him when he began
therapy were no longer distressing. Most importantly
to Mitch, however, was a newfound sense of being at
ease with himself, of being at home inside his own
skin.

I use Mitch's case to illustrate neutrality and its
potential lapses because it concerns a more subtle
manner in which neutrality can be discarded than
that often found in the clinical literature concerning
gay men. Isay (1993a) does a thorough job of docu-
menting the devastating effects that a therapist's lack

of neutrality about homosexuality can have on a gay man's treatment. In addition to this most blatant disregard for neutrality, however, there are other, more subtle, varieties. Some of these varieties may also be based on prejudice against homosexuality (as Mitch may have been communicating when he mused about the possibility that he and his previous therapist may have "spoken different languages"). Other instances of a disregard for neutrality may reflect an allegiance to a particular theoretical model with strict behavioral guidelines as to the nature of mature or healthy development. Whatever the basis of the therapist's disregard for neutrality, the result for patients, like many gay men who are prone to shame and guilt, can be an exacerbation of these affective states.

SUMMARY

Anonymity and neutrality, cornerstones of psychodynamic clinical theory from its inception, remain vital concepts in psychotherapy with gay men. However, their vitality pivots on the clinician's willingness to view them not as absolutes but as flexible and fluid.

Anonymity, especially, is best utilized if viewed flexibly. Relative anonymity is most helpfully utilized if it is measured by (1) the state of the patient's twinship selfobject development, and (2) how intrusive or disruptive a therapist self-revelation will be at a given moment. Conscientious attention to these criteria preclude self-revelations that are solely countertransferential expressions and increase the likelihood that a self-disclosure will be an empathic act, of value to the patient.

Neutrality is best removed from the position it has sometimes occupied in traditional theory as being synonymous with silence. Neutrality is most usefully defined as a sincere curiosity, an earnest desire to understand the patient's world in all its complex nuances. As true curiosity precludes judgment, viewing neutrality in this manner also militates against the therapist's imposition of his or her values upon the patient. While it is neither possible nor really desirable to completely render the therapist valueless, the maintenance of a sincerely curious approach to the patient provides the assurance that the therapist's values do not eclipse the patient's values as psychotherapy unfolds.

Flexible anonymity and neutrality, appropriately utilized, enable the psychotherapist to maintain a consistent focus on empathic immersion in the patient's experience. Combined with respect, sensitivity, and courtesy, they form an environment that allows the patient the freedom and safety to discover/create his true self.

5

Respect, Sensitivity, and Courtesy in the Relational Environment

The central task and responsibility of the therapist is to seek to understand the patient as a being and as being-in-his-world. All technical problems are subordinate to this understanding. Without this understanding, technical facility is at best irrelevant. . . . With it, the groundwork is laid for the therapist's being able to help the patient recognize and experience his own existence, and this is the central process of therapy.

Rollo May

Respect, care, and consideration are attitudes that psychoanalysis, too, requires.

Bruno Bettelheim

THREE CENTRAL COMPONENTS

Aside from the classical conceptions of anonymity and neutrality, there are a number of other interpersonal qualities that affect the psychotherapeutic environment. This chapter explores those qualities that are most important in clinical work with gay men—the levels of respect, sensitivity, and courtesy available in the environment. These three qualities, which could legitimately be proposed as components of neutrality, are considered separately and in some depth because they are central to the psychotherapist's function as a selfobject for the patient. Asserting that respect, sensitivity, and courtesy are crucial to psychotherapy has a face validity that seems so obvious that it does not even merit mention. However, when applied to the psychotherapeutic treatment of gay men (or any other marginalized group), these terms carry specific meanings in addition to their commonly held definitions (Cornett 1993b).

Respect

Respect, as it is popularly conceived of in our culture, concerns the willingness to give consideration to another, to avoid violation of another's wishes, boundaries, values, and so on. Respect in psychotherapy with gay men means this, but something more as well. True respect is grounded in the willingness to be honest—both with oneself and with the patient. The willingness to be honest, thus respectful,

is an overriding consideration in successful psychotherapy.

The psychotherapist wishing to work with gay
men needs to know honestly his or her feelings,
values, and thoughts about a range of topics. I will
present four on which successful psychotherapy
turns.

First, how does the psychotherapist feel about
gay men? What personal values come into play when
homosexuality is considered? What theoretical position does the therapist maintain on homosexuality
(i.e., is it a pathological aberration, benign developmental defect, biologically rooted phenomenon, etc.)?
Central to these questions is whether the therapist
believes that homosexuality is psychologically
chosen or biologically imposed. One will conceptualize psychotherapy with a gay man quite differently
if one views it as a chosen lifestyle rather than the
result of genetic and/or biological forces, as are eye,
hair, and skin color. It is difficult to truly empathize
with a man lamenting the pain and isolation he feels
as a result of social reaction to his homosexuality
when one believes he could have avoided or now can
escape all that pain and isolation if only he would
renounce the decision to be homosexual.

At one of this country's most respected universities, I was holding a conversation with a distin-
guished clinician wishing to demonstrate the liberal
orientation of the primarily psychodynamically oriented faculty at the institution. I asked how homosexuality was regarded by the faculty, to which came
the reply, "Oh, we have faculty and staff members
who have made that choice and we accept it." An
important and not uncommon remark regarding ho-

mosexuality, suggesting a theoretical bias that cannot avoid influencing clinical responsivity.

The second area in which the clinician must be fully aware of his or her values and feelings is sexual behavior. The psychotherapist must honestly know how he or she views sex and graphic descriptions of sex generally and homosexual sexual activity in particular. Does heterosexual intercourse seem inherently more satisfying? Are there sexual acts in which homosexual men engage that are repulsive or abhorrent? Even more basically, what is the purpose of sexual behavior (i.e., is it primarily or secondarily a procreational activity, a biological/emotional activity involving communication, affection, etc.)? One's beliefs regarding all these areas will affect the capacity to hear gay men discuss sexual conflicts, achievements, and desires.

In a time when AIDS continues to ravage the gay male community, it is imperative that a psychotherapist be able to truly hear descriptions of sex in graphic detail. It is in these descriptions that shame, guilt, contempt, and alienation often find a voice. The clinician whose capacity to tolerate graphic discussions of sex is compromised will find his or her capacity to offer the optimal psychotherapeutic environment similarly compromised.

The third area of self-knowledge necessary for successful clinical work with gay men concerns monogamy. Is monogamy the only legitimate relational goal? Does a non-monogamous relationship express a fear of commitment, responsibility, or other issues? Is non-monogamy equivalent to promiscuity? Is a non-monogamous relationship as viable or more viable than a monogamous one? This is an important area in gay men's relationships. Because gay men have fewer societal prescriptions and are more accustomed to violating societal proscriptions regarding relationships, there is much more freedom to experiment and much more support for relational experimentation in the gay male subculture. Some studies suggest that a large percentage of gay male couples maintain a non-monogamous or "open" relationship. For example, McWhirter and Mattison (1984) found that of 156 couples interviewed, only seven had maintained sexual exclusivity over the course of their relationship. How one values monogamy and conceptualizes it in relation to emotional/psychological/interpersonal maturity will have a deep impact on the environment a psychotherapist offers a gay man.

Finally, the psychotherapist must honestly know how he or she feels (perhaps most importantly) and thinks about AIDS. Is AIDS the result of homosexual "promiscuity"? Does homosexual behavior somehow cause AIDS? Is AIDS a disease like any other, striking people randomly? Is AIDS a form of retribution (i.e., either against a group of people—gay men—or against a culture) for individual or collective transgressions against the moral or ecological order? Perhaps most importantly, is AIDS spread through casual contact? After a decade of living with the AIDS pandemic, many, perhaps the majority, of people in this country are to some extent conflicted regarding the relationship of AIDS to the male homosexual community. Psychotherapists are not immune to such conflicts. Indeed, the advent of the AIDS crisis seems to have awakened a latent and virulent hatred for gay men in many people, including some psychotherapists. As a result, this is an area of his or her soul that a clinician must know to be able to offer respect as an aspect of the psychotherapeutic environment.

What I am proposing is that psychotherapeutic respect resides in the clinician's ability to offer the patient a model of someone who has searched for his or her own true self and is in touch with that self. However, more than that, the therapist must act with deliberate integrity. Each of the four areas outlined above will usually surface at some point in psychotherapy with a gay man. The psychotherapist must resolve any dilemmas inherent in these areas to respond genuinely, authentically, and thus respectfully to the patient.

I have proposed previously (Cornett 1993b) that my conception of respect involves the integrity to refer a gay man to another therapist when one cannot reconcile an affirmative view of homosexuality with one's own experience and intrapsychic world view. However, I believe it is also possible to demonstrate respect by a willingness to acknowledge openly any views one has of homosexuality so that a patient may assess whether or not the environment offered by the therapist will be of value to him. Combined with this is also an inherent act of integrity and respect in offering the patient an encounter with an authentic (and thus humanly flawed) person who can assert his or her beliefs and values, regardless of whether these will elicit love or hate (Miller 1981). Such a stance is infinitely more respectful and therapeutic than attempting to maintain a facade of accepting, affirmative imposture in dissonance with a much more powerful and authentic set of values and emotions, which are ultimately perceptible to the patient anyway.

Sensitivity

In common parlance, sensitivity has a variety of meanings when used in regard to human interaction. It can variously mean a willingness to attend to the emotions, thoughts, or conditions affecting another; a state of being "thin skinned"; or cognizance that a variety of external influences impact and shape particular groups of people. Psychotherapeutic sensitivity, while including the first of these common definitions, is largely a variation of the third usage. Kohut (1971) proposed that "the reliability of our empathy . . . declines the more dissimilar the observed is to the observer" (p. 37). Psychotherapeutic sensitivity is the attempt to narrow, through deliberate effort, the distance engendered by cultural differences between the patient and therapist, thus enhancing the reliability of the latter's empathy.

Psychotherapeutic sensitivity toward the gay male patient involves an attempted understanding of the subcultural milieus that provide the context against which his life unfolds. The gay male subculture (which is probably more accurately referred to as subcultures) is complex and varied. It is a context of symbolism and meaning distinctive from that of the larger heterosexual culture. It is incumbent upon the psychotherapist to learn as much as possible about this context.

Self psychology convincingly informs that the path to truly understanding another human being is through empathic immersion in that person's world. It has also demonstrated that this can only be fully accomplished through an existential encounter between two people—the one in search of understanding and the one attempting to understand. However, there are other, adjunctive methods of empathic immersion. One method is the study of the social symbolic world in which the person who is the object of study functions daily.

Because the homosexual man is a virtual nonentity in the symbolism and ritual of the larger heterosexual culture, it is necessary that he create his own symbolism and ritual to fulfill these needs in his life. There is also an expression of this symbolism through idiosyncratic language. The word *gay* is an example of this.

Gay began as a term that allowed homosexual men to identify themselves to each other in a code unavailable to those who might overhear a conversation and subsequently create difficulties for the parties involved. Over the years, however, this word began to take on new meanings. In the 1960s and 1970s it became a defiant and proud alternative to homosexual, which had both pejorative moral and psychological overtones. Over the past two decades it has further developed into a word with larger political meanings. The same can be said of the word *queer*. Originally an epithet hurled by those wishing to demean homosexuals, it has gradually been transformed into a word utilized by many gay men to describe themselves. The wish to rob the derisive intent of those using the word has been given expression by the co-opting of the word itself.

It is particularly important for the psychotherapist to understand the symbolism, especially the language, of the gay male subculture because that symbolism does not necessarily conform to the rules of expression in the larger culture. Because there is

such stigma attached to homosexuality in this society and because this has often necessitated secrecy,
much symbolic expression has evolved in ways that
are opposite to those in the heterosexual world. This
inversion (to use a word often used in the early and
middle decades of this century to describe homosexuality) of symbolic rules may, at first hearing, be
confusing to one unfamiliar with the milieu.

A simple example of this process is exemplified
by a manner some gay men use in referring to each
other. Many gay men refer affectionately to each
other with feminine descriptors. A gay man may be
called "girl," "girlfriend," "sister," and so on by
friends or intimates. Such phraseology is often used
to communicate comfort and safety between the two
parties of the exchange; it can be a playful communication of affection. The opposite would be true in
the heterosexual world. If one heterosexual man referred to another in feminine terms, a slight would
probably either be implied or inferred. It is hard to
imagine one heterosexual man greeting another as
"girlfriend" without offense being offered or taken.
Gay men have often taken the symbolism that has
been used to express societal contempt for them and
turned it into confirmatory symbolism.

Each locality has a gay male community with
features uniquely its own. I am not suggesting that
there is a universal way of understanding all gay
men. This, after all, would be nothing more than
stereotypy. However, it is crucial that the psychotherapist be sensitive to the differences between the
heterosexual and homosexual cultural ethos and
avoid attempting to understand the milieu of the gay
man through the lens of heterosexualism. One excel-

lent heterosexual psychotherapist, who had been treating a gay man for some time, offers an example of a lapse in sensitivity in this regard. It was nearing April 15, often a time of some anxiety in this country. The patient was describing irritation about his income tax situation. The therapist, listening intently, asked simply if the patient and his lover filed joint returns. The patient was struck by the question. Of course they had not filed joint returns. This simple act, taken for granted by the heterosexual majority, is illegal for homosexual couples. This simple, seemingly innocuous, question left the patient wondering how much the therapist he had come to trust truly understood about the societal hurdles facing gay men. This concern, which was ultimately addressed and worked through, was, however, at the heart of some disruption of the remainder of that and another session.

The tendency to view the world through a heterosexual lens can best be addressed by knowing gay men, by involvement in the activities that are attended by gay men, and perhaps most importantly, by reading the writings of gay men. Local and national popular publications, literature, and political works are especially helpful in this regard. These generally capture the important themes and concerns of the national and local gay male communities. This type of sensitivity can both offer the patient an experience of affirmation in itself and can gently, and nonthreateningly challenge the important resistance that gay men often bring to psychotherapy—the fear of having hope, the fear that they again will not be understood and valued *as gay men.*

Courtesy

In common usage courtesy refers to polite interaction. Psychotherapeutic courtesy refers to the psychotherapist's capacity not only to treat the patient with appropriate social amenities and deference, but also to value the unique and unusual circumstances that arise in psychotherapy and in which the patient finds himself.

Most theorists (e.g., Greenson 1967) note the extraordinary qualities that characterize the psychotherapeutic relationship. There are limitations as to the types and extent of interactions between the parties involved. An intense and intimate relationship develops between the parties, but it is expected that this relationship will be discussed rather than acted upon. A fee is involved. There are idiosyncratic rules that govern the behavior of the therapist and, to some extent, the patient. Psychotherapy is, in short, an unusual and inherently anxiety-provoking enterprise.

Psychotherapy research (e.g., Luborsky 1984, Strupp and Binder 1984) has consistently demonstrated that the psychotherapist who acknowledges the provocative nature of psychotherapy to the patient and acculturates him to it is more likely to achieve the goals he or she sets for the endeavor. Acculturating the psychotherapy patient is offering an experience of socialization to a special interpersonal relationship. Greenson (1967) notes that the psychotherapist's willingness to explain the rationale for the idiosyncrasies of the therapeutic relationship enhances the therapeutic alliance. With the gay man, it does a good deal more as well.

Because of the lack of socialization experiences available to him throughout his development, often culminating in a sense of being an observer on the outside, unintegrated into the culture's chief symbolic activities, the gay man is hungry for such experiences. The courteous act of explaining how and why psychotherapy is conducted in the way that it is provides a socialization experience. It is an activity that integrates the two participants into the encounter and establishes psychotherapy as a reciprocal endeavor between them (Sullivan 1954).

Simply socializing or acculturating the patient to the psychotherapeutic relationship also avoids the narcissistic injury that can be inherent in initiating a relationship with a stranger whose values, perceptions and judgments are unknown. Like silent neutrality, silence at the initiation of a therapeutic endeavor is often perceived not as acceptance but as judgment. Gay men, like other groups that are not integrated into the culture as full members, have no a priori reason to expect psychotherapy to be anything other than another, perhaps more subtle and sophisticated, experience of rejection by a psychotherapist, who, gay or not, is experienced as heterosexual (Isay 1993b). The simple act of explaining the psychotherapeutic process to a gay patient can move him from a sense of being an outsider to a sense of being a full partner. Such a move bodes well for the future course of the relationship.

HAL: AN ACT OF RESPECT

Fran was a young psychotherapist employed by a small community mental health center. Because she had very little experience in clinical work with gay men and wished to learn about it, she asked to see a gay male patient who requested services in the out-patient division of the center. Fran maintained a very relaxed and liberal attitude toward most things in life and, although heterosexual, believed that she had no values that would create difficulties in working with a gay man.

Hal, the patient she had requested be assigned to her care, was in his mid-twenties. When he began seeing Fran he expressed a desire to "settle down" and begin a monogamous relationship with a suitable man.

Almost immediately Fran began to experience "confusion" with Hal. Most confusing to her was the fact that Hal often sought out married men who were presumably heterosexual as sexual partners. When his efforts at seduction were successful the resulting affairs would be intense, secretive, and highly en-gaging initially, but they all ultimately ended in Hal's being rejected.

After her first couple of sessions with Hal, Fran dropped by my office to tell me that she was excited by what she was learning from Hal (I was involved in the assignment of the case), but also to share her confusion regarding the dilemma that Hal created for himself. We informally reviewed some possible dy-namic scenarios that might, at least partially, ac-count for Hal's self-defeating interpersonal pattern, such as self-hatred expressed through the constant search for rejection, fear of emotional confirmation of his homosexuality by sleeping only with presumably heterosexual men, and oedipally tinged triangulation expressing unresolved longings for his father (Isay

1989). Fran said that these ideas were intriguing; she thanked me and then left.

Fran saw Hal weekly and her confusion did not lessen. Indeed, it increased in intensity, matched by a growing frustration with Hal. She continued to seek my assistance, and I sensed that her confusion was blocking all exploration with Hal. Finally, during one of these impromptu supervisory sessions I suggested that her confusion might reflect a discovery that she was making about herself. Perhaps she was discovering a deeply held value that helped define her and exerted more power than she had been aware of previously.

Fran wrestled earnestly with this issue for some days. She finally returned to my office to relate that through honest introspection and soul-searching, she had discovered two important things about herself. First, she discovered a very strong value concerning monogamy that interfered in her attempts to truly understand Hal. His involvement with married men violated this value and the attempt to understand it resulted in cognitive and emotional dissonance. Second, and most disappointing to her, she discovered that Hal's "predilection" for heterosexually married men touched on a prejudiced stereotype she maintained regarding gay men—that they attempt to "recruit" or "proselytize" heterosexual men. At the very least, Hal's behavior suggested that gay men are sexually without moral scruple. She was both deeply disappointed and angry with herself that she held this belief. We talked about the possibility of moving beyond these difficulties to truly learn about Hal; with real integrity she expressed concern that she could not do so in time to be of assistance to him.

During their next session Fran very honestly and courageously presented her dilemma to Hal. She explained that she wanted to be of help to him, but was having difficulty doing so because of her own dynamics. She did not elaborate on the nature of these dynamics. While such an elaboration can sometimes be helpful, in this case it seemed to serve no real purpose and Hal expressed no curiosity about her revelation. Fran suggested to Hal that he might be better served by another therapist. He acknowledged that he had been concerned that "we weren't getting anywhere." He did, however, express concern that he had done something to offend Fran and offered an apology. This offered Fran an opportunity to point out that the difficulties of others in understanding him were neither Hal's fault nor his responsibility. By this time there was probably little doubt in Hal's mind that Fran was struggling with her own human imperfections, and was, in distinct contradiction to Hal's parents, assuming responsibility for them. Hal assertively agreed to a transfer, but requested one more session to terminate with Fran.

During their last hour together Hal expressed the feeling that he was being rejected, which in an undeniable sense he was. Fran offered the observation that this rejection also involved a triangle—she, Hal, and the new therapist. However, at that point she very skillfully differentiated the rejection that results from someone believing that another person is valuable enough to be given the best care possible—to be respected—from the rejection that results from that person simply no longer being of narcissistic convenience. Hal responded thoughtfully to an idea that seemed clearly alien to him. He related a sense of understanding that Fran did care about him on a very basic level and that this rejection was an act of integrity on her part, with his welfare clearly in the forefront of her mind.

Hal worked effectively with the new therapist and related that the referral from Fran had been painful and initially reminded him of never "being good enough," but that he understood the difficulties to be hers, not his, and ultimately accepted her referral as an act of respect, affirming his importance and value.

Fran was surprised by the discovery she had made about herself through her work with Hal and decided that entering her own psychotherapy might be appropriate. She subsequently did so.

It is worth noting that this vignette represents an extreme on the continuum of demonstrating respect. Most acts of respect do not result in referrals or countertransference disclosures. However, through this extreme example the value of much smaller acts of respect may be demonstrated. Additionally, the extreme nature of the example suggests that even a treatment situation requiring the psychotherapist to discontinue the treatment as an act of integrity and respect can have felicitous results if skillfully carried out.

KEVIN: A FAILURE IN SENSITIVITY AND COURTESY

Kevin was a 37-year-old gay man who requested psychotherapy from a social service agency and was assigned to a young, gay, male clinical social worker named Bill, who was under my supervision. The intake information provided to the therapist asserted that Kevin had a long history of unstable interpersonal relationships and some history of substance abuse/dependence; he had experienced periods of acute depression requiring hospitalization and was intermittently suicidal. A final note on the intake form said simply "Probably BPD," the abbreviation for borderline personality disorder.

Armed with this information, Bill met with Kevin for the first time. He acknowledged later in supervision that he had entered this first hour with Kevin convinced that Kevin was probably "a borderline." At that point in his professional life Bill was deeply interested in the theories of Masterson (Masterson 1976, Masterson and Klein 1989) and Kernberg (Kernberg 1975, Kernberg et al. 1989) regarding borderline personality disorder. He was convinced that his initial priority must be the establishment and maintenance of a "secure frame."

As Kevin entered the office Bill introduced himself, using only his last name. Kevin introduced himself, using only his first name. Without further introduction, Bill then informed Kevin that he had received and read the intake worker's note. He then fell silent.

Kevin, appearing anxious, stammered, "What should I talk about?"

"Whatever seems important to you right now," was Bill's reply.

Kevin then expressed concern that he really did not know how to address Bill. Bill questioned Kevin as to how he would like to address him and Kevin stated a desire to be on a first-name basis. (In supervision Bill related that this desire seemed "too familiar—a lack of boundaries.")

The remainder of the first session was punctuated by silences and frustration—Bill carefully attempting to avoid giving out "too much information" and Kevin seemingly stymied by the ambiguity of the situation. Bill came to supervision convinced that he was already assuming the role of "bad object" in what he was sure was Kevin's rigidly bifurcated world view.

Initially, Bill and I discussed the ubiquity of splitting to the human condition—and especially to the gay human condition. Bill, a sincere and committed social activist as well as psychotherapist, asserted this view to be a homophobic faux pas on my part. We discussed the larger social milieu that makes splitting a necessary aspect of homosexual survival. Such splitting is often represented in the difficulty that psychotherapists who are politically attuned have in reconciling the fact that gay men demonstrate both the expectable developmental characteristics that have been pathologized by some theorists (e.g., splitting) and artifacts of development in a hostile culture (Kimmel 1978) with the fundamental view that these characteristics and artifacts in no way suggest more psychopathology than that present in the general populace. The reasonable unwillingness to accept homosexuality as a pathological condition has also sometimes led, especially with young therapists, to a rejection of *differential* developmental dynamics between homosexual and heterosexual men. This seems to entail another instance of difference being treated as inferiority.

Bill and I also discussed his belief that he needed

to set such firm boundaries with Kevin. He linked this with the theoretical models he found of particular interest. It could also be added, however, that one of the most deleterious facets of diagnosis had entered the picture. After reading the intake information, and one session with Kevin, Bill was certain that he was dealing with a man who had BPD. We looked at the initial environment he had offered Kevin and the narcissistic injury and frustration involved in an environment that is so ambiguous that it demands almost complete vulnerability. I encouraged Bill to acculturate Kevin to the process of psychotherapy and offer him basic information such as how he wished to be addressed. Such basic courtesies are invariably helpful in inviting a patient into a meaningful relationship. I invited Bill to consider use of first names. Psychotherapy is an enterprise best served by the use of first names. It is, after all, a very intimate experience for both participants. The use of titles and last names often erects a false boundary that only serves to block intimate communication (Strean 1988).

Bill returned to his next hour with Kevin and implemented the suggestions we had considered during his supervision. He broadly described the process of psychotherapy and his belief regarding how and why it worked. The second session witnessed a decrease in the tension of the atmosphere and Kevin became more relaxed and related the concerns of his life more easily.

During the third hour with Kevin, Bill faced challenges both to his anonymity and his capacity to maintain a respectful approach to Kevin. It was during this session that Kevin asked him directly if he was homosexual. Bill, caught unaware, defensively demanded to know Kevin's fantasies about this question. Kevin provided no elaborate fantasies, instead stating simply that he sought assurance that Bill "could understand where [he was] coming from." Receiving no acknowledgment from Bill, but feeling the press to talk anyway, Kevin went on to describe a recent sexual encounter that had been disturbing.

Kevin was interested in mild sadomasochistic (S/M) sex, mostly dominance-submission scenarios and mild bondage. Bill later recounted feeling revulsion toward the activities that Kevin spoke of. He also found himself ignorant of much of what Kevin described; Silverstein (1991, 1993) notes that adherents of S/M sex maintain a subculture separate from even the male homosexual subculture. At one point during the hour Kevin described having oral sex with his partner who did not wear a condom (this apparently heightened the effect of the scenario being enacted). He related that the most disturbing aspect of the encounter, however, had been his fantasy/wish that his partner, a man he had not known before that night, would tie him and anally penetrate him to orgasm without a condom (this had not in fact occurred, however).

Without allowing Kevin to develop the motivations for this wish so that the dynamics underlying it could be understood, Bill launched into a lecture on safer sex. He informed Kevin in no uncertain terms that unprotected oral sex was risky enough, but that unprotected anal sex "should be out of the question." (Feeling guilty, Bill did inform Kevin, however, that whether or not he practiced safer sex was his decision, thereby discharging his obligation to allow

Kevin a measure of self-determination.) Bill wanted to be certain that Kevin had the facts that "could save his life."

This session, and with it Kevin's therapy, ended on this note—without exploration of what his fantasy could have meant. Bill acknowledged that over the course of their three hours together Kevin probably learned very little about himself. Bill, too, had no real idea of who Kevin was.

In supervision, Bill and I reconstructed a portion of his reactions in this session. In the guise of maintaining anonymity Bill had refused to answer Kevin's question regarding his sexual orientation. However, closer examination revealed that this defensive refusal was actually founded on shame. Bill acknowledged being frightened of the agency administration's reaction if it was discovered that he was revealing his sexual orientation to patients. There may have been some validity to this fear, but whether completely accurate or not, it can be surmised that Bill's reaction communicated a great deal to Kevin. Although certainly not intentionally, this act of "maintaining anonymity" almost surely communicated to Kevin that homosexuality is something of which one should be ashamed.

Bill also acknowledged that he did not understand Kevin's interest in S/M sex and found it difficult to tolerate his talking about it. Although he did not understand much of the symbolism and ritual involved in the fantasies and practices of this style of sexual relation, he did not seek out any further understanding of it. While this represents a serious interference, it also represents a not uncommon lapse in therapeutic sensitivity. Even among gay male therapists, who have experienced such lapses of sensitivity throughout their lives, there is a tendency to try to make every patient's cultural experience accommodate itself to the therapist's world view. Again, although not intentional, such smugness does not serve the process of psychotherapy well.

Finally, Bill had difficulty tolerating Kevin's fantasy of unprotected anal sex. He originally proposed that he wished to impart information to Kevin, which he believed that Kevin might not have. However, after exploration of his reaction to this fantasy during the session it became apparent that the shame and self-hatred involved in unprotected anal sex with a stranger was overwhelming to him. He had treated Kevin disrespectfully by lecturing him because the fantasy touched again upon his own shame and because it touched on unresolved grief from the deaths of several of his own friends.

The experience with Kevin invited Bill to return to his own psychotherapy. He paid heed to this invitation and this experience served as a catalyst for him to learn much about himself. Unfortunately he, and I as his supervisor, probably allowed much too much of this learning to have occurred at Kevin's expense.

SUMMARY

In addition to the capacity to maintain neutrality, the psychotherapist must maintain an attitude toward the patient characterized by respect, sensitivity, and courtesy. While these words all have meanings in their common usages that make them applicable to dynamic psychotherapy with gay men, they have some specific meanings in the context of psychotherapy as well.

Each of these terms signifies the striving for a specific type of empathic interaction. Respect is the capacity to move beyond, as much as is humanly possible, one's own self-deceptions; to know, and if necessary, communicate the values one holds that will interfere with optimal responsiveness to the patient's true self. Sensitivity is the psychotherapeutic willingness and ability to seek an understanding of the patient as part of a sociocultural and symbolic context. This is not done to categorize, typologize, or stereotype the patient; sensitivity is reflected by those acts of the therapist that focus on understanding the patient in a larger context. Sensitivity eschews stereotypy. Finally, courtesy embodies those acts of polite interaction to which the patient is entitled as a human being. It is also reflected in a specific attitude on the part of the psychotherapist that acknowledges the extraordinary nature of the process of psychotherapy and acculturates the patient to that process. Courtesy not only lessens the needless anxiety of the patient regarding the circumstances of treatment, but invites him to become a full and equal partner in the enterprise.

Respect, sensitivity, and courtesy, both singly and in combination, are quiet challenges to the fear of hope, the foundation of most "resistances" in clinical work with gay men (Cornett 1993b). These three qualities, combined with therapist neutrality, simultaneously create the safety of the psychotherapeutic environment and quietly invite the patient to discover/create his true self. Each of these qualities forms a portion of the atmosphere that nurtures and sustains the patient as he struggles to find what is authentic in him. In the safety of this environment, transference phenomena can then assume a position of prominence.

6

Transference

It is a method destined to bring to light . . . the subjective choice by which each living person makes himself a person; that is, makes known to himself what he is. Since what the method seeks is a *choice of being* at the same time as a *being*, it must reduce particular behavior patterns to fundamental relations—not of sexuality or of the will to power, but of *being*—which are expressed in this behavior.

Jean-Paul Sartre

In psychoanalytic *theory*, the concept of transference serves as an explanatory hypothesis, whereas in the psychoanalytic *situation*, it serves as a defence for the analyst.

Thomas Szasz

The so-called transference which for Freud represents nothing but a reproduction of the infantile, becomes a creative expression of the growth and development of the personality in the therapeutic experience.

Otto Rank

TRANSFERENCE: A COMPLEX CONCEPT

It is one of Freud's chief accomplishments that he recognized the centrality of the relationship between the psychotherapist and the patient to the treatment experience. Transference, the core relational construct of psychoanalysis and psychodynamic psychotherapy, has been elaborated over the history of the psychoanalytic movement probably more than any other. Theorists and clinicians have struggled with every aspect of the concept. Such basic areas as defining transference, operationalizing it, and the extent of transference in psychodynamic psychotherapy, including whether there is a dual "realistic" relationship versus a "transference" relationship operating in the psychotherapeutic encounter, have been the focus of study and disagreement (Greenson 1967, Schafer 1983, Solomon 1992c). At present, there is no universally accepted definition of transference (Giovacchini 1987).

This chapter first offers a conceptual and historical context for transference, and then constructs a view of transference that maximizes its usefulness in clinical work with gay men. Finally, a clinical vignette is offered to illustrate this view.

TRANSFERENCE IN AN HISTORICAL CONTEXT

Transference was first "discovered" as Josef Breuer treated Anna O. (Breuer and Freud 1895). During this treatment Anna O. developed a deeply eroticized longing for Breuer and Breuer became terrified. He told Freud, a junior colleague and friend, of this situation. As an observer rather than participant, Freud had the distance to form an intellectual perspective on this phenomenon. As Breuer fled from his patient's longing, Freud began to hypothesize about the psychological dynamics of the case.

Freud tentatively explained Anna O.'s transferential longing for his colleague in contradictory ways, depending on his audience. To Breuer he offered the possibility that the patient's intense emotional reaction was founded upon her internal dynamics, projected onto a kindly and compassionate physician treating her. This reassured the frightened Breuer who held himself in some measure responsible for his patient's erotic yearning.

To his future wife, Martha, Freud expressed the belief that Anna O.'s reaction required an attractive man, like Breuer, as a catalyst, thereby reassuring her that he would not be pursued by lovesick patients throughout his career (Szasz 1994b). Interestingly, Freud's contention that Breuer would be more apt to be the focus of erotic transference longings was based on his view of himself as unattractive, having too many features traditionally considered Jewish (Menaker 1989). It seems that at least a part of his first formulation of transference was colored by self-hatred.

Like all of his thinking, Freud's ideas regarding transference evolved and developed over time. In the earliest days, during his collaboration with Breuer, Freud conceptualized the curative element of psychotherapeutic treatment to be the emotional catharsis that resulted from the expression of long-forbidden wishes and memories. Transference was seen as a resistance, perhaps the most potent resistance, to the cathartic process. Transference phenomena served to protect the patient from recognizing the repressed trauma that, when uncovered and emotionally experienced, liberated him or her from neurotic suffering. This view of transference is logical in light of what actually transpired in the treatment of Anna O.—her strong attraction to Breuer frightened him enough to result in termination of her treatment.

As the cathartic conception of psychotherapy evolved into the psychoanalytic, Freud's (1912a) thinking concerning transference evolved as well. Although still seen as a resistive hindrance, transference phenomena came to be viewed as important information regarding the patient's instinctual functioning. However, with the construction of the Oedipus conflict as the foundation of the psychoanalytic edifice, the conception of transference as a manifestation of instinctual life was supplanted by its conception as an expression of unresolved oedipal conflicts and yearnings. In one form or another classical psychoanalysis and dynamic psychotherapy accepted this oedipal conception of transference as a basic starting point.

Intrinsic to these early understandings of transference was the idea that it represented a distortion of the *real* person of the therapist and the *real* relationship between therapist and patient. Because of the therapist's relative anonymity and neutrality, transference was seen from this perspective as being constructed upon qualitative distortions of reality (Blanck and Blanck 1974, Moore and Fine 1990e). Although much else has been discarded by contemporary dynamic clinicians, many retain this view of transference. Kubie (1975), for instance, proposes that

> the purpose of [transference analysis] is to make clear
> to the patient what parts of his conscious feelings are
> appropriate and what parts inappropriate, and how
> these feelings have arisen out of earlier relationships.
> This is of great value to the patient because it shows
> him how such transplanted feelings have the power to
> distort other human relationships. [pp. 92–93]

The difficulty with this view of transference phenomena as both oedipally based and as distortions of
reality became apparent as analysts and psychotherapists began to treat patients whose psychological
development had arrested prior to the oedipal period.
These patients clearly demonstrated transference
phenomena, although they did not form stable transference neuroses. Further, these very primitive patients also demonstrated the almost uncanny ability
to tailor their transference reactions to actual characteristics of the clinician. Faced with this dissonant set
of facts, object relations theorists expanded the notion of transference to include the projection of the
contents of the patient's psychic repository of relational development onto the person of the therapist
and emphasized the importance of the actual therapist as a full participant in the process (Kernberg
1980). Although originating in the treatment of very
disturbed patients, this view of transference is attributed by current object relations theorists to the full
continuum of patients seen by psychotherapists
(Strupp and Binder 1984).

The American interpersonal school, a variation of the object relations tradition, took as its foundation Freud's (1912a) understated observation that transference is based on some realistic, existent quality in the psychotherapist. Interpersonal theorists (e.g., Gill 1982, Winer 1994) propose that transferential interactions concern the patient's elaboration, or perhaps more accurately *overelaboration*, of actual aspects of the therapist's character and personality. In the interpersonal tradition, the distortion involved in transference does not involve the quality of a given therapist characteristic (e.g., as projection in the classical conception of transference would), but the quantity of it present. For instance, a psychotherapist may have sadistic elements to his or her personality that, while not necessarily overtly identifiable, are perceived by the patient in interactions. Transference elaboration would then involve the magnification of this quality as characteristic of the primary experience with the therapist. Distortion of the relationship, then, occurs not through simple projection of the patient's internal world onto the receptive blank screen therapist, but through magnification of existent qualities in the actual therapist that give tangible substance to the patient's developmental experiences (Winer 1994).

The interpersonal perspective on transference illuminates the importance of the therapist maintaining an acute understanding of his or her anti-homosexual prejudice. (I include in this description gay male psychotherapists whose anti-homosexual prejudice can present itself as shame resulting in sustained empathic lapses toward the patient.) Striving for anonymity, relative or otherwise, does not hide such prejudice, and the propensity to conceptualize transference as a projection-based distortion of the "real" therapist allows the therapist to deny the existence of such prejudice. While such a conception of transference allows the therapist to deny his or her own anti-homosexual bias as having an impact on the psychotherapy, it does not in fact prevent that bias from having a negative impact on the patient. Winer (1994) makes this point well:

> It seems plausible, at least, that in those treatments where the analyst needs to deny his personal impact on the process, patient and analyst will collude to keep a great deal more from view than would otherwise be necessary. Since all the patient's perceptions are also founded on transference—the transference having found its point of attachment at the present reality—paradoxically the effort at keeping a clean field obscures the transference. [p. 28]

Influenced by the object relations and interpersonal traditions, Kohut (1971) began to formulate a conceptualization of transference phenomena with patients deemed to have narcissistic characterological problems. However, over the remainder of his career, Kohut (1977, 1984) came to assert this view of transference as clinically ubiquitous. He essentially proposed transference to be an interpersonal process that has important intrapsychic functions but is distinctly reality based. He proposed that the need for a cohesive and coherent emotional and psychological world, embodied in the self, is the primary psychological need of life. It takes precedence over all other psychological or emotional needs. To maintain cohesion and coherence, the person makes use of others as extensions for weaker or more vulnerable parts of the self. Persons performing this service are selfobjects. The use of selfobjects is a universal aspect of human development and functioning that continues throughout the life cycle. Indeed, Kohut believed the person to be inseparable from his or her selfobject milieu or matrix (Wolf 1988). Selfobjects are utilized to maintain narcissistic equilibrium in all the spheres of the self (i.e. mirroring, idealizing, and twinship) and if a particular sphere is deficient, selfobjects will be utilized to bolster it.

For Kohut, transference was more accurately described as a compensatory process rather than a process of projection and displacement, founded on compulsive relational repetition. Thus, for Kohut, viewing transference as a distortion of the therapist–patient relationship was inaccurate. Instead, the patient seeks to make use of the psychotherapist as a selfobject, to fill deficits in his capacity to maintain emotional and narcissistic equilibrium.

Kohut (1984) favored a more basic view of most clinical phenomena, including transference. He preferred to think of clinical processes as less complex than the classical view of complicated unconscious defenses and arcane symbolism (e.g., Goldberg, in an interesting interview with Hunter [1994], discusses Kohut's lack of conviction that parapraxes, traditionally held to convey rich information about the patient, actually had any clinical utility). Instead, the "manifest" material of the patient and the experience of being with the patient communicated the nature of the transference without impenetrable formulations of sequences of drive–defense–and so on.

Kohut's view of transference is preferable in working with gay men because it obviates one potential pitfall of theories of transference that propose distortion of reality to be the primary element. Szasz (1994b), for instance, argues that the differentiation of "real" from "transference" relationships relies on the inference and interpretation of the clinician. This, of course, is subject to error. Indeed, countertransference reactions will actively influence the clinician's judgment regarding what is transference and what is not (Giovacchini 1987).

An error of judgment regarding whether a patient's reactions to the clinician are "realistic" or "transferential" can be an empathic lapse with painful consequences for the patient. Being told that one's perceptions are faulty or that one's feelings are inappropriate or are reactions to misperceptions is painful, no matter how such a pronouncement is delivered.

Additionally, Szasz proposes that transference can be employed as an explanation for phenomena arising in the therapeutic dyad that protects both parties from an encounter with the authentic personality of the other. This is a provocative idea with important ramifications for the understanding of the psychotherapeutic process. Specifically, if the psychotherapist is striving to provide an environment that will allow the patient to explore/create his genuine identity, then a concept that is founded upon the notion that the patient will actively, albeit unconsciously, distort the relationship, and that these distortions can only be identified and defined by the therapist, presents an important incongruity. Kohut's conception of transference, while proposing

that the clinician can identify transference phenomena, has the advantage of also maintaining that these
phenomena are responded to as realistic assertions of
the patient's wants, needs, and so on. Responsiveness of this sort amplifies the patient's identity,
rather than arbitrating it as a focus on interpreting
relational distortions often does (Cornett 1993a).

It is also noteworthy that classical conceptions of
transference are founded on the idea that a patient's
psychopathology is essentially neurotic in nature,
with little narcissistic complication. For some years
that description of the typical psychotherapy patient
has been growing less accurate (Van Der Leeuw
1980). Certainly with gay men it is impossible to
dismiss the significance of narcissistic injury in the
development of the basic difficulties that propel them
into psychotherapy.

Finally, Fromm (1980) also critiques the classical
view of transference as relational distortion. He links
this conception of transference with a social structure
that strives to maintain its hierarchy by encouraging
childlike helplessness through the arbitration of "reality" and the "appropriateness" of feelings engendered by social interaction. As a corollary of this
Fromm suggests "that the more real the analyst is to
the analysand and the more he loses his phantomlike
character, the easier it is for the analysand to give up
the posture of helplessness and to cope with reality"
(p. 41).

A CONCEPTION OF TRANSFERENCE
WITH GAY MEN

The object relations and self psychological perspectives inform an understanding of transference phe-

nomena with gay men. These perspectives also provide the foundation for an approach to clinical work with such phenomena. As I proposed above, of most importance is the fact that these two perspectives eschew the classical notion that transference represents a distortion of the real relationship between the two therapy participants. Instead, both these models assume that the development of the patient's transference is in response to actual characteristics of the therapist and the therapeutic environment.

In psychotherapy with gay men it is helpful to conceptualize transference phenomena as simultaneously having two coexisting levels. Following Kohut's model it is helpful to view the first level as a compensatory one. On this level the patient utilizes the psychotherapist as a selfobject to compensate for deficits in one or more spheres of the self. In essence, the patient makes use of the therapist to stabilize a functional identity structure. This process involves the patient's demonstrating his typical manner of maintaining internal equilibrium and an accustomed identity. On this level the patient reacts to one or more actual characteristics of the therapist to initially complete his identity. For instance, the therapist's mirroring responses provide completion and temporary stability to an identity prone to shame-based fragmentation. The therapist's willingness to be idealized allows the patient to merge with his or her strength and to calm himself in the face of narcissistic injury through reliance on this strength. Finally, the therapist's twinship selfobject responsiveness allows completion of the patient's identity by connecting him to the rest of humanity—by demonstrating that aloneness does not necessarily coincide with absolute alienation. Not every patient will experience each of these transference needs equally. For some, one transference yearning will predominate, with only fleeting glimpses of the other two. For other patients, transference needs will alternate in more equal measure.

It is crucial to note that on this compensatory level, the patient is always striving to complete himself. Transference is not simply the fulfillment of a compulsion to repeat. It is an act that seeks the achievement of wholeness of identity. It must also be noted, however, that the effort the patient places in using the psychotherapist for this goal is generally focused on maintenance of the accustomed identity, often the false self.

To alter an accustomed identity the patient must be allowed to feel a stability to his emotional and psychological life, free from fragmentation. As psychotherapy progresses, he can explore his internal world without fear of massive, overwhelming discontinuity. Those characteristics of the therapist that originally completed the self and remain desirable can also then be acquired through incorporation.

I am not suggesting, however, that the patient always utilizes an empathic characteristic of the therapist for completion of his identity, only that he initially grasps one that is *syntonic* with his view of himself. For instance, he may utilize the therapist's hostility or sadism to maintain a view of himself as worthy only of contempt or loathing. This dynamic explains some of the "successes" of sexual reorientation therapists. This type of therapy capitalizes on the patient's hatred of himself. The therapist's subtle, sometimes unexpressed, occasionally even unacknowledged, hatred for the patient's homosexuality is syntonic with the patient's contempt for his own identity. It is important to remember that a therapist's responses can be syntonic to the patient's world view and experience without being remotely empathic.

On the second level of transference phenomena, the narrative level, the patient offers a history of and explanation for how his accustomed identity developed. Essentially, the patient tells his story. As he does so, he offers a narrative explanation of the basis for the compensatory transference phenomena. He elaborates the reasons that the characteristic or set of characteristics upon which he fixed were of importance. He describes an environment in which these characteristics figured prominently, either because of their absence (i.e., truly empathic resonance) or because of their presence (i.e,. the syntonic negative resonance) in his developmental environment. The patient essentially narrates/enacts the drama of his life story, utilizing qualities of the authentic therapist as a context.

This narrative level of transference most closely resembles the classical conception of transference, although there is one important difference between the two. The classical conception focuses on the misperceptions and distortions that the patient creates against the context of an optimally anonymous therapist; the conception I offer echoes not only the self psychological tradition, but also the interpersonal and existential traditions in its assertion that the psychotherapist is never unknown to the patient—no matter how intensely anonymity is pursued. The patient fixes upon a characteristic, or most often a set of characteristics, of the authentic therapist to explain his story. If the therapist maintains a belief that the patient's reactions are a distortion of the reality of the relationship, he or she will miss that story.

THE EXPECTATION OF REJECTION

Freud's conception of transference as resistance has applicability to the gay man especially as resistance represents a fear of hope. As noted in Chapter Three, the gay man is often deeply frightened of his hope. He internalizes the rejecting stance assumed by our culture toward homosexuality. This often leads to the generic expectation that those who interact with him will be rejecting. This expectation often colors early interactions with the psychotherapist and would be broadly conceptualized as "negative transference" by some. I do not embrace a description of this dynamic as transference, however, because the expectation of rejection is generic—it does not necessarily build on actual behaviors or attitudes of the clinician.

If the psychotherapist is subtly or blatantly rejecting, this expectation of rejection can grow into a transference phenomenon that tends to become the entire experience of psychotherapy for both the patient and the clinician—an experience that neither invites the patient to explore his authentic identity nor encourages him in this endeavor if he chooses to do so. However, this expectation of rejection does not become a transferential preoccupation if the therapist is not in actuality devaluing or dismissive of the patient's homosexuality.

It must be noted that I am not suggesting that lapses of therapist empathy are not painful. Indeed, the patient remains highly sensitive to such lapses and they offer narcissistic injuries that result in moments of painful fragmentation. However, unless the therapist is genuinely contemptuous or unaccepting of the patient, these lapses do not come to define the totality of the experience with the therapist. With a psychotherapist who is accepting, neutral, and otherwise empathically attuned, occasional empathic lapses offer the patient an opportunity to strengthen his own internal self-regulatory responses. Kohut (1984) termed this process *transmuting internalization*. Essentially, the patient recalls, during moments of the therapist's empathic failure, previous successes the therapist has achieved in remaining empathically responsive. The patient uses these memories to comfort himself. Eventually, this process assumes a more permanent place as a daily part of the patient's life. It then forms an essential part of the patient's willingness to treat himself more understandingly and less judgmentally.

If the therapist's general responsiveness to the patient is colored by a rejection of his homosexuality, then the experience with the therapist will be an amplification of the rejection the patient has experienced with the larger culture. Instead of moments of empathic lapse against a background of empathic responsiveness, the opposite experience will predominate. The patient's transference will remain collusively unexplored by both participants and therefore an unresolvable resistance. Transference in this case does become a resistance that utterly blocks the patient's hope and results in a redoubling of the efforts focused upon bolstering the false self. Under these circumstances psychotherapy becomes a complex process of sadistic (the therapist) masochistic (the patient) acting out, with little real potential gain for the patient.

TRANSFERENCE AND CLINICAL TECHNIQUE: AMPLIFICATION OF THE TRUE SELF

Psychodynamic technique has traditionally focused on the systematic delineation and interpretation of transference as the sine qua non of effective clinical responsiveness. The thrust of clinical effort has been on interpretive work, with relegation of non-interpretive interactions to the category of insignificant clinical utility. Gratification of transferential longings has been actively discouraged or overtly prohibited. Blanck and Blanck (1974), for instance, admonish that "all but the most disturbed patients need more to correct their distortions than they need a real object in the therapist" (p. 187).

Kohut's (1984) view of the clinical process radically challenged the position that interpretation is the sole or predominant mutative factor in psychotherapy. Indeed, his understanding of the curative process of psychotherapy asserted that a complex variety of factors converge to make psychotherapy successful. Kohut, like Freud, Winnicott, and Sullivan, could be quite warm toward patients, engaging in interactions with them well outside the realm of interpretation (Elson 1987). He did not dismiss noninterpretive activities with patients as unhelpful. Instead, he proposed that it is the psychotherapist's capacity to perform as an empathic selfobject that determines the outcome of a treatment endeavor. Although not necessarily employing Kohut's developmental or metapsychological constructs, other dynamic clinicians have begun to move away from the position that interpretation alone is helpful and are assigning a much larger role to the relational qualities and interactions between psychotherapist and patient (Casement 1991, Meissner 1991).

It is my position that effective dynamic psychotherapy with gay men is predicated on the clinician's ability to perform as a reliably empathic selfobject. Such an empathic performance can take many forms. Its broad features make up the attitudinal environment the therapist offers, including his or her willingness to tolerate being used as a selfobject (not always easily done). It is through this responsiveness as a selfobject to the patient's compensatory transference that the psychotherapist enables the patient to functionally complete his identity. Kohut (1984) proposed that it is through the processes of selfobject function and transmuting internalization that the psychotherapist offers the patient the opportunity to permanently strengthen the structure of the self. Through internalization of the therapist's attitudinal approach to him, and also through employment of his own developing capacities for self-soothing via the process of transmuting internalization, the patient generally assumes an attitudinal stance toward himself characterized by respect, empathy, and understanding.

Responding to the narrative level of the patient's transference, the psychotherapist functions as an empathic assistant to the patient as he discovers/creates his true self. As the patient recounts his story the therapist amplifies rather than interprets this story (Cornett 1992b, 1993a). The aim is not to discern some presumably deeper meaning in the patient's material, but is instead focused on simply offering the patient an avenue for truly hearing his story, free from censure. The goal could be likened to adjusting the picture on a fuzzy television screen. The program being viewed is not essentially changed, but simply grows clearer without the distraction of interference.

As a part of this process of amplification the therapist carries out a number of activities. He or she first maintains an awareness of how the patient's story is being cast around his or her characteristics or qualities. As patterns in this area become clear, the therapist points them out to the patient. Crucial to this aspect of the therapist's responsiveness is his or her ability not only to accept and acknowledge his or her realistic personality and character as the foundation upon which the patient erects his transference, but to be capable of illuminating the ways these characteristics figure in the patient's developmental narrative. It is one proposition to assume that a patient's transference is a distortion of reality and point out to him how and in what measure it is so. There is a great deal of protection against narcissistic vulnerability available to the therapist in such a stance (Szasz 1994b). It is an entirely different proposition to assume that a patient's perceptions of the therapist are, at least to some important extent, accurate representations that have been chosen from the totality of one's personality and character to illustrate the particular nature of the patient's development. Instead of struggling against these perceptions the therapist must instead use them to amplify and illustrate the patient's narrative.

I have also found that attention to this aspect of transference informs reconstruction of the patient's developmental epic. Reconstruction is far more important in the treatment of gay men than interpretation. Because of the early denial necessary to survive as a homosexual person in our society and the alienation from the self that is the consequence of this denial, the patient often has much difficulty in offering a complete emotional history. An important part of the psychotherapist's role in amplifying the patient's story is to help fill in gaps by using the clues that the patient offers both through the compensatory and narrative transference phenomena. Through reconstruction of the patient's story, as completely as possible after the fact (i.e., especially the emotional details that have been dismissed or devalued), the patient begins to gather a full, more complete picture of himself as a complex, richly textured, and multifaceted being, the understandable result of his development. There is then often no further need for the false self and he can embrace the authentic characteristics, qualities, feelings, thoughts, and history that are at the base of his identity.

MEL: AN UNCOMFORTABLE TRANSFERENCE

Mel was a 30-year-old gay man who sought psychotherapy because of periods of depression and social withdrawal. Although these periods had occurred throughout his life, they had begun to intensify and posed a threat to his employment. He found it difficult to motivate himself for his work as a salesman, which involved constant interaction with the public. Particularly difficult were the instances of rejection he received making "cold calls" (i.e., sales calls not solicited by the intended customer).

Mel presented for his first appointment appearing slightly disheveled, dejected, and weary. Beneath this outer layer of affect appeared to reside a rage seeking expression. He described his symptomatology and immediate life situation impassively. He seemed most distressed about the peril he perceived his job to be in. With this in mind, I asked him toward the end of this first session about the utility of a referral to a physician for medication. For the first time during that hour Mel seemed to come to life.

"Medication? Do you think I'm *that* crazy?" he demanded, a look of pain and rage mixed in his eyes. Before I could respond he asserted, "No, no, no—no drugs! If there's one thing I learned from my father it's that all this mental health crap is for pansies. I'm not sure why I'm even here." His voice trailed off and he slumped in his chair, as if all the animation had been siphoned out of him.

Knowing I had blundered and seeing an opening, I quietly said, "My suggestion hurt your feelings. It seemed like I was saying that you are too weak to handle your feelings on your own. Although it was not my intention to be hurtful, I obviously was and I apologize for that."

Mel looked up, searching my face, connecting for the first time with my eyes. He responded in a quiet but firm voice, "Okay. I was also concerned that you really don't want to see me as a patient."

"That a referral to a physician might be a way of dumping you?" I asked to ensure that I understood his concern. He nodded his assent. "I'm not aware that I want to dump you—I was thinking of the referral as an addition to psychotherapy, not instead of it." This somewhat ambiguous reply was purposely phrased in this way. I was not so much attempting to correct Mel's perception of my suggestion of a referral to a physician as a rejection as to communicate that this was not my conscious understanding of it. I have found it helpful to respond to perceptions of me and my motivations for certain actions or lack of action with reference to what I am aware of. This keeps both the patient and me focused on two important ideas: first, that there may be aspects of our interaction of which I am not fully aware—and that I realize this and will monitor it. I believe this to be only logical with my conception of transference and the therapeutic process. And second, that there are dimensions to human experience that are initially out of one's awareness. This simple acknowledgment by the psychotherapist initially sets the stage and in later periods of the process reinforces the possibility of psychotherapy as an experience of discovery.

Mel appeared reassured. He declined the referral for a medication evaluation, but accepted an offer of psychotherapy. We scheduled a regular weekly hour.

After this session I thought a good deal about his perception of the medication referral offer as an attempt to reject him. I wondered if indeed I did not want to work with this man, or, perhaps more importantly, if I did not want to deal with the depth of his pain and rage—probably crucial aspects of his authentic identity. Was the suggestion of a medication evaluation a suggestion that we disguise his authentic experience? I do not agree with the oft-held psychoanalytic view that medication interferes with the process of psychotherapy. Indeed, for a patient who is severely depressed, medication often frees the motivation that makes psychotherapy possible (see Wolf [1988] for a discussion of this issue).

As I pondered the possibility that this referral, so early in my acquaintance with Mel, represented a rejection, I was also aware of very positive feelings for him. More than that, I felt an easy empathic connection to him. I fully understand the kind of depression that Mel described, because I, too, am susceptible to it. After much soul-searching, several questions remained. Was this early interaction between us an artifact of his expectation and anticipation of rejection? Was it an early clue to the nature of his narrative transference emerging? Or was it my desire to avoid working with him?

The answers to these questions, like most questions in psychotherapy, were not quickly forthcoming. Over the first few weeks of our work together, what was forthcoming was a look at how hungry Mel was for mirroring affirmation. During most of these early sessions I was offered little opportunity to speak, and when I was offered such an opportunity, only a response that very closely mirrored Mel's immediate mood was attended to. If I strayed even a little from his mood, or did not capture it exactly, a distant look would appear in his eyes and he would clearly withdraw his attention. It became apparent that one important selfobject function I would serve on the level of the compensatory transference was as a source of mirroring.

As the initial weeks grew into months I began to become aware of a vague sense of boredom with Mel. Soon I recognized the boredom for what it was—a way of masking anger with Mel. Almost as quickly as I was aware of it, so too was he. During one session, near the sixth month of his therapy, he confronted me with his awareness of my reaction to him.

"You know," he began, "I don't think you really like seeing me. In fact, I think it's hard for you to even sit here with me."

"Oh?" I asked noncommittally. "What do you think that's about?"

"You don't like having to listen to me. No, you don't like having to *really* listen to me."

Drawing on my experience with Mel, as well as what he was saying, I tried to clarify his perception. "You mean I don't like having to keep you aware of how closely attuned I am?"

"Yeah," he acknowledged. "It's like you begrudge me the attention."

The context of Mel's narrative transference came alive for me at that point. Mel had offered only a sketchy history of his family and development thus far. However, an important theme returned to at any point that he did talk about his early life was his sense that his parents, but especially his father, became angry with him and rejecting whenever he sought praise or affirmation. Instead of offering him a moment of glory, they would lecture him about the impropriety of boastfulness or bragging. His parents came across as very hungry people who had not

gotten enough of what they needed in terms of affirmation and they resented having to offer any to their
son. I, too, had begun to resent having to respond so
affirmingly to Mel, having to "work so hard," as he
put it. Like Mel (and most gay men I know), I can
experience a hunger for affirmation that seems to
have a desperate quality to it, as if there is only so
much affirmation to go around, a very limited quantity, and any of it that others get deprives me. Mel had
found a characteristic that I shared with his parents
and we could now understand his and their world
much better.

He pressed me to respond to his perception.
"Well . . . are you angry with me?"

"I think you've picked up a resentment about
acknowledging you, about affirming you as valuable
enough to be listened to carefully and completely. It
seems to be a resentment that is familiar to you. One
that you probably grew up with."

With this Mel became both angry and saddened.
He said that he shouldn't be "so demanding," that "it
is wrong." He responded to my acknowledgment of
his perception by attacking himself as his parents
would have.

"Or," I countered, "maybe you are naturally
entitled to feel that what you have to say is important
enough to be heard. Maybe when people become
resentful of your wish to be seen as valuable it is
because of their own difficulties, whether it be me or
your parents."

Mel appeared surprised. After a silence that
seemed to be filled with an earnest thoughtfulness on
his part, he related that he had not been aware of
anyone previously responding to him in this way.

The idea that a yearning for acknowledgment and affirmation might be a natural part of life was a novel one. Over the next several weeks he came to express the understanding that his hunger for mirroring had been so attacked by his parents that he wished it not to be a part of his identity and attempted to dismiss it as often as possible.

Also during this period of his therapy Mel came to understand the role that his homosexuality had played in his view of himself. Aware very early of his "differentness" from the males around him, Mel had come to link his homosexuality with the condemnation he received both for asserting himself and for the hope that he would be affirmed. This understanding emerged through attempts to systematically reconstruct his early emotional life.

Mel was often at a loss in attempting to describe early, emotionally laden interactions. An example of the role that reconstruction played in illuminating his narrative transference occurred in the ninth month of therapy. He was describing an interaction with his father when he was 6 or 7. The memory concerned his attempt to hug his father after a sporting event. He was feeling excited and wanted to share this with his father. His father rebuffed the affectionate advance, perhaps embarrassed that the interaction had occurred in the midst of a group of people. He scolded Mel and informed him that the "right kind of men" did not hug or kiss other men, even close relations. Mel's father had a vast number of rules that differentiated the "right kind of man" from the "wrong kind" and expressed these to his son at any peripherally plausible opportunity. (This may have signified that, as Isay [1989] proposes, Mel's father had become aware of his son's homosexuality and, frightened by it, sought to stamp it out.) Mel surmised after the event that the rejection he suffered was the result of his homosexuality. However, he was surprised, and somewhat confused, when I suggested that we pursue the emotional result of this rejection.

"What do you mean, how did it feel?" he said with some irritation. "I'd just screwed up—again."

"That's what you thought about it at the time," I offered. "I would think you must have felt embarrassed, hurt, and angry that he'd rejected you in front of these people."

"Why would I feel any of that? I was used to that kind of response from him."

"I doubt any human being gets used to that kind of rejection, no matter how often it happens. Especially a young boy, wanting his father's approval and notice after performing for him. I imagine that what you were accustomed to doing was dismissing the pain you felt in such interactions with him."

Gradually, through dozens of such interactions between him and me, Mel began to understand the complex affective life he had pushed out of his experience because it was simply too painful to endure on a continual basis. He also began to link these feelings with similar feelings arising in his work with me. This was poignantly exemplified in an interaction with me around the end of the second year of therapy.

Some months earlier a local paper had done a short profile of my lover and me. The article emphasized that we had a large number of pets. This provided the context for an interaction between Mel and me that illustrates patients' uncanny ability to build transference reactions around real characteristics of a therapist. Mel had been describing a particularly difficult day, one filled with rejections from potential clients. I was attempting to remain neutral and also sought to echo the level of frustration and pain he experienced. He became silent and then confronted me.

"There's something that's been bothering me for a long time," he began. "Can we talk about it?"

"Sure," I responded with some surprise that he felt the need to ascertain my willingness to discuss *any* subject.

"I don't think you really care about me. I think you sit and listen, because I pay you to do that. I think you'd rather be anywhere but here. You do a good job of *acting* interested in me, but you really aren't. In fact, I don't think you really like people. I think you like animals much better than you do people."

I had to sit and contemplate what he said for a moment. In the abstract he was absolutely correct. I much prefer the company of animals to that of people. However, in that moment with him I was aware of being genuinely interested in him—and caring very much about his pain. I finally responded, "Mel, that's an important perception of me and I appreciate very much the courage it took to share it. It is also an accurate perception on one level. I do enjoy animals as a general rule more than I do *people I don't know*. I'm not aware that that disqualifies me from really caring about you. Perhaps. . . " I began but was interrupted.

"Perhaps you're not like my father," he said with a quiet excitement that often accompanies an important understanding of oneself.

"Perhaps not," I rejoined.

He went on to talk about a fantasy that I like animals because I get "tired of listening to bitchy fags all day." However, as soon as these words left his mouth he smiled and acknowledged the internalized hatred of such a comment. For the first time in his therapy, Mel suggested that he could feel my interest in him, but was frightened of believing it.

Over the next year Mel became aware of the many nuances of feeling that were a part of his life. With the experience of finally feeling that another person could appreciate and value his experience, he began to appreciate and value it as well. Through our interactions involving my confirmation of his perceptions of me, he seemed to develop the capacity to accept that there is a complicated variety of feelings and values that make up a person, many of them often in contradiction. He explored these aspects of himself, learning gradually to value his complexity.

Mel's therapy ended after three years. He was much calmer and more confident. He had changed jobs and now worked for a company that genuinely appreciated him. He was placed in charge of representing this company with the gay community, a position he greatly enjoyed. He dated when a man seemed interesting, but felt no compulsion to have a lover. Most importantly, he related that the experiences of fragmentation that had characterized his depression had dramatically lessened. He had learned much about himself, not all of which he liked, but all of which he accepted as natural, authentic, and valuable because it was a part of his core identity.

SUMMARY

The analysis of transference has been considered the foundation of psychodynamic technique since Freud's seminal elaboration of the topic in 1912. Over the past eighty years much has been written about transference and transference analysis. In this chapter an attempt has been made to integrate and synthesize some of the more recent thinking regarding transference into a conceptualization that is of optimal benefit to gay men. This attempt has liberally utilized self psychology and interpersonal theory, although the result is surely existential and neither of these models would easily embrace it.

In psychotherapy with gay men all technical activities are subordinated to one goal: creation of an environment that affirms the patient and invites him to discover/create his authentic self. Clinical work with transference serves this goal as well. By understanding transference phenomena as attempts to complete the functional identity and to explain the development of that identity through utilization of characteristics of the therapist's authentic identity, the psychotherapist offers the patient an opportunity to clarify his values, attributes, and feelings, the essence of his distinct individuality, in juxtaposition to those of the therapist.

This conceptualization of transference militates against viewing the patient's reactions to the therapist as projections or other distortions of reality. Indeed, this conceptualization of transference challenges the psychotherapist to know him- or herself as intimately and genuinely as possible. It offers extended and extensive opportunities for narcissistic vulnerability. Freud (1905) captured this quality well when he proposed that psychotherapists who truly struggle with their patients to discover the meanings of their lives cannot "expect to come through the struggle unscathed" (p. 109). However, the psychotherapist willing to tolerate this vulnerability offers an important, perhaps unique, opportunity for the patient. Almost equally important, though, is the opportunity the psychotherapist is offered to experience the depths of his or her own identity and to grow as both a clinician and a human being.

7

Countertransference

The danger of intellectualization is all the greater today, when the prevailing alienation from one's own affective experience leads to an almost total intellectual approach to oneself and the rest of the world.

Erich Fromm

A person who has consciously worked through the whole tragedy of his own fate will recognize another's suffering more clearly and quickly, though the other may still have to try to hide it. He will not be scornful of others' feelings, whatever their nature, because he can take his own feelings seriously. He surely will not help to keep the vicious circle of contempt turning.

Alice Miller

THE UBIQUITY OF COUNTERTRANSFERENCE

The role of the psychotherapist's affective life in psychotherapy has always been considered of dramatic importance. In early psychoanalytic theory countertransference was considered a parallel phenomenon to transference. Just as the patient utilizes the therapist via displacement and projection to recreate childhood conflicts, the psychotherapist, when responding countertransferentially, was thought to be engaged in the same type of interaction. For this reason, countertransference was initially thought to represent weaknesses in therapists' training, especially in their training analysis, and therapists were loath to admit that countertransference played a role in their clinical work. Currently, therapists' willingness to acknowledge the impact of their countertransference on the process of psychotherapy is considered a hallmark of professional maturity (Burke and Tansey 1991).

What transpired between the early conception of countertransference and the contemporary conception followed a similar evolutionary path to that of transference. Through the work of object relations, interpersonal, self psychology, and existential theorists, the importance of the psychotherapist's affective contributions to psychotherapy has been emphasized. This chapter briefly reviews the evolution of countertransference as a clinical construct and then focuses on countertransference phenomena specific to clinical work with gay men.

A WORKING DEFINITION OF COUNTERTRANSFERENCE

Freud's thinking regarding countertransference has been interpreted in a variety of ways, and has been offered as support for widely divergent perspectives on the (mis)uses of countertransference in psychotherapy (Moore and Fine 1990b). Indeed, there seems to be a continuum in the psychodynamic literature related to the manner in which countertransference is employed in clinical work with patients.

On one extreme of this continuum are those who believe that countertransference represents eruptions of the therapist's psychopathology. For those on this extreme, countertransference is best dealt with through self-analysis and, if this is not successful, through a return to psychoanalysis or psychotherapy.

On the other extreme of the continuum are those who believe that countertransference encompasses all the feelings that the psychotherapist experiences in working with a patient. These emotional responses are seen as at least partly, if not primarily, facilitated by the patient's psychopathology. Theorists on this end of the continuum maintain that countertransference reactions to a patient offer valuable information about that patient's psychopathology and the impact that the patient has on others in his or her interpersonal milieu.

As in most other things, probably the vast majority of clinicians fall toward the middle of the continuum with a marked preference toward one end or the other. However, the analogue of the continuum highlights the importance of defining what is meant when the term countertransference is employed and avoiding the assumption that practitioners enjoy a common definition and understanding of the term (Moore and Fine 1990b).

As the term *countertransference* is employed in

this chapter it occupies a middle position on the continuum, referring to the psychotherapist's use of the patient to meet selfobject needs. This, however, is not equivalent to considering all countertransference reactions to be manifestations of the therapist's psychopathology. Selfobject needs and the fulfillment of these needs are an integral, indeed inseparable, aspect of the human condition. Rather than considering the use of the patient as a selfobject for the therapist as a manifestation of the therapist's psychopathology, I prefer to look at the impact that the patient functioning in this capacity has on the process of psychotherapy. This impact can be relatively benign or neutral, relatively positive, or relatively negative. It is important to emphasize the relativity of each of these descriptions because utilization of the patient as a selfobject with a primarily negative impact may have positive features and vice versa. Similarly, a primarily benign or neutral impact may have positive and/or negative features. This can be illustrated through three scenarios in which a patient meets mirroring selfobject needs for the therapist.

An example of a relatively benign or neutral use of the patient as a mirroring selfobject is the patient's payment of the fee charged by the psychotherapist. The therapist charges a fee and expects the patient to pay it. In addition to its practical survival value, the fee is a source of professional affirmation for the therapist, confirming that he or she is offering something of value to the patient. By paying the fee the patient fulfills a mirroring selfobject function for the therapist.

A relatively positive utilization of the patient as a mirroring selfobject often occurs during a patient's utilization of a therapist as an idealized selfobject. The patient idealizing the therapist fulfills a compensatory function for himself. Merging with the idealized psychotherapist (as merging with an idealized parent would have done during childhood) offers the patient an opportunity to bolster his self-esteem and manage his anxiety through a sense of connection to the idealized qualities of the therapist. However, this idealization also serves a mirroring selfobject function for the therapist. To be treated as if one's words are absolute wisdom provides powerful affirmation to the clinician. The therapist's toleration/enjoyment of this situation is also very beneficial to the patient in need of a selfobject to idealize. For the therapist to reject the patient's idealization would result in narcissistic injury to the patient and disruption of the psychotherapeutic process.

A relatively negative utilization of the patient as a mirroring selfobject occurs when the psychotherapist must continually demonstrate his or her superior insight through brilliant interpretations (this is an inherent danger of reliance on interpretation in psychotherapy). The patient's willingness to marvel at the therapist's perceptive acuity and intuition provides a mirroring experience for the therapist. However, because this most often transpires at the patient's expense, especially in terms of his or her own sense of competence and achievement, it is generally short-lived. Gay men, accustomed to a culture that touts its superiority over them, will tolerate such a situation longer than some other groups of patients, but will ultimately leave such an experience, albeit often without acknowledgment or perhaps even awareness of why they are doing so.

COUNTERTRANSFERENCE VULNERABILITIES OF GAY MALE PSYCHOTHERAPISTS WORKING WITH GAY MALE PATIENTS

Having defined countertransference as the psychotherapist's use of the patient as a selfobject, the impact of which can be either relatively positive, negative, or neutral on the process of psychotherapy, it is important to note some potentially negative countertransference pitfalls to which gay male psychotherapists working with gay male patients are particularly vulnerable. These include the therapist's use of the patient to confirm a shame-based false self, reliance on the patient to meet excessive mirroring needs, and reliance upon the patient to meet social needs or other excessive twinship needs.

In the discussion of anonymity in a previous chapter, the notion was offered that anonymity may at times function as a cover, albeit an opaque one at best, for the psychotherapist's shame regarding his own homosexuality. The psychotherapist may attempt to cover his shame in other ways as well. Isay (1993b) notes one of the most common in his discussion of the tendency of some psychotherapists to tacitly encourage gay male patients to view them as heterosexual. As Isay proposes, many, if not most, gay men begin psychotherapy with the assumption that their psychotherapist is heterosexual. This is a reflection of their own shame and the internalization of a powerful societal prejudice against homosexuality. For patients, psychotherapists are often fantasized (and sometimes purported) to be paragons of mental health. It is difficult to see them as part of a class of people regarded by many in the culture as pathological. Under optimal circumstances this fantasy gives way to a more accurate view of the clinician. The gay patient will experience his gay therapist as flawed in the ways that all humans are flawed, but as a person no different, neither better nor worse, than he. As he comes to understand the humanity of the therapist, he often similarly comes to understand his own humanity, with all its rich and complex nuances, ambivalences, and contradictions.

A difficulty arises, however, when the psychotherapist views his homosexuality as pathological and experiences shame regarding it. Under such circumstances, he may collude with the patient's heterosexual assumption about him by never exploring it, let alone challenging it. This type of passivity is often ostensibly maintained to protect the therapist's anonymity, but it generally functions to maintain a false self that offers some relief from that shame. A psychotherapy characterized by such a shame-based collusion does not offer the patient an opportunity to experience the therapist's full humanity, or his own. The patient's opportunities to experience himself as a being who is understandable, to search the multiple emotional, interpersonal, and psychological nuances that form his authentic identity are sacrificed to the maintenance of the therapist's false self.

Another danger, based broadly on the therapist's shame, is that the patient will be used to meet excessive mirroring needs for the therapist. This can transpire through the psychotherapeutic technique itself, especially when this technique is founded upon interpretation. Gay psychotherapists experience the full range of contempt and loathing to which gay men are heir in this culture. As a result, they are often vulnerable to fluctuations in their self-esteem that can result in moments of fragmentation. The process of psychotherapy, with its inherent frustrations and disappointments for both participants, can potentiate this vulnerability.

The danger in any psychotherapy that assumes that the psychotherapist has some secret knowledge or the key to some understanding that is unavailable to the patient is that the psychotherapist will be raised to an unrealistically exalted position. A psychotherapy that purports to rest extensively on interpretation heightens this danger. Such a situation provides much affirmation to the therapist through the mirroring responses of the patient, but also, if left unchecked, ultimately robs the patient of the opportunity to experience the therapist's imperfect but understandable humanity and, through it, his own.

A third countertransferential danger hinges on the therapist's use of the patient to meet excessive social needs (i.e., as a twinship selfobject). Psychotherapy can be an isolated profession. It is by nature secret and unavailable to public discussion. These qualities can heighten any twinship vulnerabilities latent in a gay psychotherapist and intensify his sense of himself as alone and alienated from the rest of the culture. Isay (1993b) notes that one potential outcome of this situation is that the therapist may use the patient as a source of social fulfillment, thus abrogating the sometimes onerous responsibility of psychotherapy in favor of a pseudo-friendship. This state of affairs can leave the patient feeling exploited because he is, after all, paying for the experience. It can also reinforce the notion that his only value is based on what he can do for others.

Closely related to this potential pitfall is another, which involves the psychotherapist utilizing the patient as a twinship selfobject for the purpose of confirming the therapist's basic sense of himself as connected to the rest of humanity. Under these circumstances the therapist uses the patient not necessarily as a friend but as a sounding board for his own functioning. This type of countertransference difficulty is characterized by high levels of therapist self-disclosure, advice-giving, and so on, which is not necessitated by the patient's material and, indeed, is overwhelming to the patient. Patients accurately perceive this type of countertransference difficulty as the therapist's search for identity confirmation, which, by its very nature, interferes with their own.

Avoidance of the latter two countertransference pitfalls requires the psychotherapist to maintain a social network of friends and colleagues outside the consulting room. In addition to the support of colleagues and friends, an ongoing supervisory relationship, and, especially at times of high stress, his or her own psychotherapy, provide the therapist the best protection against turning the process of psychotherapy into an endeavor that subjugates the needs of the patient to the needs of the therapist.

Having offered a definition of countertransference as the psychotherapist's employment of the patient to fulfill selfobject functions, I now offer a conceptualization of the remainder of the clinician's emotional involvement in the process of psychotherapy. This can be done initially by looking at the ambiguous concept of abstinence.

ABSTINENCE

Another aspect of countertransference considered in the dynamic literature is the therapist's overall emotional involvement in the process. Considering any and all, especially intense, reactions to the patient as countertransference is probably related to Freud's ambiguous and often contradictory admonitions regarding abstinence (Gay 1988).

Freud seems to have been conflicted regarding the role he believed the psychotherapist's emotions play in the process of psychotherapy. In some instances he encouraged therapists to maintain the distance and objectivity of a chess player or surgeon (Freud 1910, 1912b, 1913). At other times he equated psychotherapy with love and intimated that this quality accounted for the curative properties of the endeavor (Bettelheim 1982, Gay 1988). For many, abstinence came to be associated with the former description, and was viewed as the mature psychotherapist's emotional posture toward the patient. Given this association, it is logical that the psychotherapist's experience of emotional involvement, especially intense emotional involvement, would be considered countertransference.

For much of the early part of this century psychodynamic clinicians, with the notable exception of Ferenczi, favored the view of therapist emotional reactivity and responsiveness as countertransference. It was not until after Freud's death that countertransference, and more specifically the therapist's affective reactions to the patient, came to be viewed as anything but a hindrance to treatment (Sandler 1976).

However, as with so many other aspects of psychodynamic theory, necessity brought innovation. As analysts and therapists began treating patients with more significant psychopathology, character analysis became the desired rather than avoided route of treatment. As this occurred, the value of the clinician's emotional responses to the patient clearly asserted itself. Gradually, over the past forty years, the literature on countertransference has overcome discussions as to whether or not the therapist's emotional responsiveness represents the need for further psychoanalysis. It has now progressed to discussions of the uses and meanings of this responsiveness and when and how much of it should be revealed (Burke and Tansey 1991, Frederickson 1990, Lomas 1994).

Perhaps the most important area to be considered when exploring the relationship between countertransference and psychotherapy with gay men is the interaction between the two identities involved in the enterprise. These identities are both asserted in large measure through affective responsiveness. The therapist's affective responsiveness then plays an extremely important part in the psychotherapeutic process. When viewed from this perspective, abstinence must assume a different guise than has often been the case in the psychotherapeutic endeavor.

ABSTINENCE AND IDENTITY

The primary difficulty that the concepts of countertransference and abstinence have posed for psychotherapy involves confusion, especially for novice psychotherapists, in the differentiation between *experiencing* emotional reactions in work with patients and *acting out* those reactions destructively. Avoidance of destructive therapist acting out toward the patient is imperative. However, the complete avoidance of experiencing emotional reactions is impossible, and even if possible would inevitably lead to acting out. Nevertheless, novice dynamic psychotherapists often attempt to maintain an emotionally detached posture toward their patients (perhaps as near an approximation as possible of the passionless involvement of a surgeon or chess master).

This state of affairs offers significant problems for a conception of psychotherapy that considers identity to be of paramount importance. It encourages the psychotherapist to regard his or her own emotional responsiveness, the most intimate aspect of identity, as suspect in clinical work. It also encourages the therapist in the erection, maintenance, and protection of a false, albeit professional, self.

For the gay man, or indeed for a member of any other group who is struggling to establish and maintain contact with an authentic identity, such a stance by a psychotherapist neither invites nor sustains attempts to achieve this contact. Psychotherapists must be in continual and intimate contact with their feelings. If they are, these feelings can provide the foundation for a variety of therapeutic functions. However, the most important function served by the therapist's respect for the importance of his or her own affective responses to the patient is the presentation of a model of authenticity and full integration (or as near to this as is humanly achievable). The patient will perceive this authenticity and integration in every moment of the process, even if the therapist never voices these feelings directly. There is no more effective means of demonstrating the centrality of affect to identity and inviting the patient to acknowledge and respect his feelings as an inseparable and rich part of his unique identity.

Beyond providing a model for patient identification, the clinician's ability to maintain intimate contact with his or her own affective responses serves a variety of other important functions. Primarily, the therapist's emotional responses serve to permit more accurate identification with the patient's emotional life and thus inform empathic responsiveness to the patient. These emotional responses also inform an understanding of the possible affective reactions that others may have to the patient, thus supplementing an understanding of the patient's compensatory and narrative transference reactions.

ADDRESSING EMOTIONAL RESPONSES THAT HINDER CLINICAL WORK: THE ISSUE OF DISCLOSURE

Currently the most controversial area in the literature on countertransference concerns how the psychotherapist should address countertransference when it has had a negative impact on psychotherapy (Burke and Tansey 1991). Specifically, the issue of whether to acknowledge countertransference to the patient as the basis for clinical blunders is hotly debated.

Traditional dynamic psychotherapists often maintain that countertransference-based reactions are best analyzed by the clinician alone, with a supervisor, or, if need be, with his or her own therapist or analyst. Seldom, however, *if ever*, is it appropriate for the psychotherapist to review countertransference difficulties or dilemmas with the patient, according to this perspective (Arlow 1985, Brenner 1985).

Over the past two decades this perspective on countertransference has been increasingly challenged. Building on the notion that the psychotherapist's affective/countertransferential reactions to a patient may re-create the reactions that others in his interpersonal milieu have when interacting with him, some theorists have convincingly argued that the sharing of one's affective/countertransferential reactions may form an effective interpretive intervention (Frederickson 1990, Lomas 1993, 1994). Others argue that the therapist's affective/countertransferential reactions are influenced by the patient's projective identifications, for which the therapist serves as a container (Ogden 1982). Disclosure of these reactions can at times serve an empathic function. Indeed, some clinicians have proposed that responses by the therapist to the patient, widely considered a priori signs of destructive countertransference (e.g., sarcasm, frank expressions of anger or hatred), can actually be signs of intimate empathic attunement (Frederickson 1990, Ruvelson 1988).

These arguments have a great deal of validity. However, I think the most compelling argument for the judicious disclosure of affective/countertransferential reactions, especially in clinical work with gay men, hinges on identity. As has been noted previously, affect is one of the key elements of identity—and one of the first elements suppressed when it does not match the expectations of others. The psychotherapist's willingness to disclose his or her own affective reactions to the patient accomplishes a number of diverse things. It communicates the therapist's lack of fear regarding his or her feelings and invites the patient to approach his own feelings similarly. It also offers a model to the patient of another person attempting to differentiate identity based on emotional states; this also subtly challenges the notion that one must accommodate feelings to the expectations of others.

In short, judicious disclosure of the therapist's emotional reactions to the patient, broadly considered countertransference, can serve multiple functions, including aiding the patient in understanding his own emotional world and the impact that his actions can have on the emotional responses of others. These disclosures can also offer a model of authenticity that eschews a fear of feelings—no matter what those feelings may be.

APOLOGIES

Another area of controversy in discussions of the functions and handling of countertransference concerns apologies. Again, there is a dichotomy of thought: some clinicians maintain that apologies are never helpful to the process of psychotherapy, and some propose that, at proper times, apologies are quite facilitative of effective psychotherapy (Goldberg 1987).

The potential danger of apologies to patients has generally been seen to reside in the possibility that a clinician may employ a patient in a role that is detrimental to him (e.g., as a confessor, or as a source of gratification for the clinician's masochistic tendencies). The logical extreme of this position holds that *any* apology represents a potential danger and is thus best avoided.

I strongly agree that a psychotherapist must not use a patient as a source of absolution or for the enactment of a scenario that features the therapist's masochism. However, it is often helpful to acknowledge with an apology empathic lapses one has allowed to occur with a patient as a result of one's own emotional distraction or unavailability. An apology for an empathic lapse that has painful consequences for the patient is a deeply empathic act of rectification. It not only communicates that the therapist is aware that his or her actions have consequences for the patient (something narcissistically impaired parents may not have ever communicated), but it directly communicates that the patient's experience is of primary importance. An acknowledgment of error and apology can also disincline the gay male patient to view the therapist as a superhuman creature, above making mistakes, to whom the patient can never realistically hope to feel comparable. Having argued for the importance of maintaining a flexible view of apologies that does not devalue and dismiss them out of hand, I also wish to note some caveats that are best observed in this regard.

First, I agree with Solomon (1992a) that apologies must also be explored to ascertain the impact that they have on the patient's dynamics. Because the clinician offers a sincere apology does not mean that it is interpreted as such by the patient. Apologies may have been a source of manipulative guilt induction in the patient's past.

Second, too many apologies present problematic dynamics. An overabundance of apologies defeats an important message that can be communicated to a patient in an effective psychotherapy. This message involves the understanding that perfection is impossible and that all failures to reach perfection are to be treated as sources of shame or guilt.

Finally, as with any other therapist disclosure, the therapist must use as a guide the motivation of the considered apology. The therapist's need to apologize as part of a pattern of atonement for generalized guilt or shame is not helpful to the psychotherapy process. Indeed, such an apology deflects the attention of the session from the patient to the therapist and may place the patient in a position of feeling the need to provide nurturance to the clinician. Similarly, an apology that forms part of a complementary interpersonal pattern involving the acting out of masochistic and sadistic elements is also not facilitative of effective psychotherapy.

As is the case with the motivations for most interactions that occur between patient and therapist, the complete motivations for the latter's behavior may not be fully known to either participant. The therapist may not be cognizant of destructive motivations for apologies or of any other form of affective/countertransference disclosure. The hallowed notion of maintaining vigilant and careful internal supervision and self-analysis, augmented by external supervision and periodic psychotherapy or psychoanalysis, offers the most comprehensive method for minimizing potential countertransference disclosures that subjugate the patient's needs to those of the therapist.

NATHAN: USE OF THE THERAPIST'S EMOTIONAL RESPONSIVENESS

It would be impossible to delineate, much less describe, all the types of emotional response and reaction that a clinician can encounter in the course of practice. However, I offer an example from fairly early in my career (when I still struggled with understanding abstinence and the role of the psychotherapist's authenticity in psychotherapy) of the role that the therapist's affective responses can play and the impact that disclosure of these responses can have on therapy.

Nathan was a 42-year-old gay man who consulted me for psychotherapy after the breakup of a long-term romantic relationship. During our first session he expressed resentment about the relationship's demise. Nathan was deeply secretive about his homosexuality. He was especially resentful of the fact that he would now be forced to search for homosexual companionship and that this would entail risk. He believed that his job, a very lucrative and highly visible position, would be jeopardized if his homosexuality became public knowledge. Although he and his lover had lived together for years, he maintained a belief that the larger heterosexual community knew them only as "roommates" and he deeply resented the dilemma now before him: to seek out companionship and risk exposure as a homosexual, or to maintain his secret and endure some degree of loneliness.

After my first meeting with Nathan I found my-self irritated with him. I have seen and continue to see a large number of homosexual men who keep their sexual orientation a secret to some degree. Although I maintain a strong belief that our culture would be more accepting of homosexual people if all homosex-uals were open regarding their sexual orientation and also hold as an important personal value my open-ness as a gay man, I have not found this problematic in working with men who see this issue differently. I do not generally find my neutrality compromised because of this. Yet, with Nathan I experienced re-sentment that he would keep his sexual orientation a secret to keep his job, at a cost to other homosexual people—and ultimately himself.

Initially, I focused on the possibility that my resentment originated in some unresolved residue of my own shame. Perhaps I envied the financially lucrative nature of his work and the prestige that this offered. I also internally explored the possibility that my resentment represented an empathic connection to his frustration toward both his lover and a culture that values him only as long as he remains inau-thentic in his functioning. These possibilities seemed incomplete—there was more to it.

Over the first three sessions it became increas-ingly difficult to attend to Nathan. He spent most of these hours detailing his fears that if he attempted to date he would be discovered and, as a result, lose his job in abject humiliation. I found myself increasingly distracted, considering things outside the therapy during his hours. At times, I entirely lost the thread of what he was saying.

As the fourth session began with Nathan, I determined to break this emerging and disturbing pattern. As I listened to what seemed like the same complaints I had heard ad nauseam, I suddenly realized something and impulsively confronted Nathan with it, almost cutting him off in mid-sentence.

"You know, Nathan," I began, "I've heard you talk a great deal about how your breakup has left you vulnerable to being 'outed,' and how distressing this is for you, but I have not yet heard you express any sadness about the loss of the man who was your partner."

This observation certainly seemed accurate and may have been an area that Nathan would wish to explore. However, he clearly had not focused on this aspect of his breakup at that moment. My confrontational comment was not empathic in any regard, and almost as soon as the words left my mouth I was aware of the discounting, even contemptuous, manner in which they had been expressed.

Nathan initially looked wounded, but then a growing sense of rage became discernible. "Yes?" he challenged, his voice betraying a sharp edge of anger.

I sat stunned. I was not sure where to go with what had become an obvious blunder, expressing only my hostility. I decided to pursue a safe course, but one that also offered the potential for rectification. I offered my perception of his evolving affective state.

"My comment seemed to hurt you and my sense is that you are now angry with me," I offered.

"I don't know about being hurt, but I *am* angry with you."

I was appreciative of his assertiveness and his desire to be genuine with me, perhaps more genuine than I had been with him. "Can we talk about that?" I asked.

"What, my anger?" he asked more tentatively.

I nodded.

"It just seemed like you were judging me. My relationship had been over for a long time before the breakup—I was resigned to that. It's like you were calling me selfish or something. I've heard that all my life but I didn't expect to hear it from my therapist." Despite these words, Nathan sat looking at me with an expression that seemed to suggest a resignation to being judged and labeled by everyone.

"I appreciate very much your honesty. And I don't have the right to judge you, nor do I really have the desire to judge you. But despite that it seems I did and I apologize. That was a hurtful thing for me to do."

A light came back to Nathan's eyes and he seemed appreciative of my attempt to repair the rupture in our relationship.

I continued, "In hurting you today, it sounds as if I added to the hurt of many years."

Nathan went on to detail several moments in his development during which he felt shamed and hurt as his parents labeled every consideration for himself "selfish," "self-centered," or "egotistical." He had experienced his lover as doing much the same thing throughout their relationship.

My reaction to Nathan became much more comprehensible to me in light of this information. It had involved the re-creation of a familiar interpersonal pattern for Nathan, which included projective identification. However, it was built on my flawed assumption that I could simply and completely compartmentalize portions of my identity with the unwarranted conviction that this would never have an impact on my clinical work. Further, I had fallen into a dangerous pattern of disingenuousness with Nathan, which he corrected with his forthrightness and authenticity—a case of the patient treating his psychotherapist (Searles 1990).

Nathan's treatment ultimately reached a conclusion with which he was satisfied. My irritation with him dissipated after our interaction regarding my judgmental comment.

I grew up with an oft repeated maxim, "Do as I say, not as I do." Nathan, however, impressed upon me the importance of congruity and authenticity for the therapist. This is a lesson that has been reiterated many times since.

SUMMARY

Countertransference is the therapist's utilization of the patient as a selfobject. This is a natural and unavoidable part of psychotherapy. However, this utilization may have relatively negative, relatively positive, or relatively neutral consequences for both the patient and the psychotherapeutic process. The therapist must carefully monitor the impact of countertransference and, to the extent possible, minimize its negative impact.

Another aspect of the therapeutic interaction that has traditionally been labeled countertransference is the psychotherapist's emotional reactivity and responsiveness to the patient. I prefer to qualify this description of countertransference because it has led to confusion in the conceptualization of abstinence and has resulted in Herculean, if nevertheless ineffective, attempts to constrain the therapist's emotional involvement in the process of psychotherapy.

The therapist's emotional reactivity to a patient can richly inform the work with that patient in a multiplicity of ways. One's emotional responsiveness to the patient can facilitate the patient's acceptance of himself as a complex being with rich emotional nuances deserving of understanding. For a psychotherapy that views identity as pivotal, as psychotherapy with gay men is best advised to do, the psychotherapist's capacity to both react and respond emotionally to the patient is crucial.

Psychotherapy is a process filled with discovery and creation for both patient and therapist. Countertransference and, more broadly, the therapist's emotional involvement in the process may be the vehicle by which the therapist learns about him- or herself. In addition to the importance of our own authenticity and emotional integration, a crucial lesson that this involvement may offer is a humility that keeps every patient unique and worthy of our consideration and attention.

8

Beyond the Office

Awareness refers not only to the uncovering of inner conflicts but equally to conflicts in social life that are negated and harmonized by ideologies (social rationalizations). Since the individual is a part of society and cannot be conceived of outside the social fabric, the illusions about social reality affect the clarity of his mind and thus also prevent him from liberating himself from the illusions about himself.

Erich Fromm

A LIFELONG JOURNEY

Throughout this book I have argued that effective psychotherapy with gay men pivots on the concept of identity. I have presented the discovery/creation of the authentic self as if it is a result or destination. This may be a little misleading, and it calls for clarification. The discovery/creation of the authentic self is a lifelong journey. It is a process, rather than a result. It is not achieved when psychotherapy ends—

no matter how successful one or both parties believe that the experience has been.

What psychotherapy offers a patient is usually a start on this journey. The psychotherapist serves as a companion and, at times when the terrain becomes unsure, a staff. However, when formal psychotherapy ends, the patient's process of discovery and creation continue. One ingredient of successful therapy, then, is the kindling of a fire in the patient to see himself as an evolving being, to view himself with respectful awe and fond curiosity. Fromm (1976) describes this quality: "The essential factor in psychoanalytic therapy is this enlivening quality of the therapist. No amount of psychoanalytic interpretation will have an effect if the therapeutic atmosphere is heavy, unalive, or boring" (p. 23).

If the therapist and patient kindle such a fire together, another hunger generally develops in the patient—a hunger to see authenticity in the environment around him and, indeed, in the world at large. Fromm (1976) goes on to propose that with a hunger to know what is authentic in ourselves, we become hungry to know what is authentic in others. This hunger leads to an unwillingness to accept the convenient, the superficial, and the societal status quo.

THE PSYCHOTHERAPIST'S CHALLENGE TO BE A SOCIAL ACTIVIST

I have observed many patients during the process of psychotherapy who become unwilling to accept the treatment offered to gay men in our society. They become activists, although not necessarily in the sense that the political and religious right employ that term. They become activists in the sense that they become active in the pursuit and promulgation of authenticity—the nearest we as humans probably come to Truth. This activism decries the perspective of gay men as socially, morally, legally, or psychologically inferior to heterosexual people. This type of activism in our patients is a challenge to us as psychotherapists to take up this form of activism.

Traditional psychodynamic clinicians have shied away from a social activism that would take them out of their offices (although as I am proposing, much activism in patients can be created and sustained through the relationship that develops in that office). Arguments have been offered that the visibility inherent in social activism has deleterious effects on our patients. By some accounts (e.g., Masson 1990), some psychoanalytic clinicians have even refused to allow photographs to be taken that might be used publicly, out of a fear that this public exposure might negatively contaminate their clinical work.

There is much to be respected in the argument that we must be vigilant regarding the effects our involvements outside the office can have on patients. Such involvements are provocative and their impact on patients should not be dismissed as unimportant for exploration and understanding. If these involvements are in some way hurtful, this, too, should be acknowledged and, if possible, rectified. However, a posture of social passivity is equally provocative, especially for psychotherapists who work with homosexual people. To simultaneously maintain a philosophy that genuineness and authenticity are qualities to be valued and to remain passive in the face of societal condemnation of, and discrimination against, people who acknowledge and assert their identities is incongruent. This incongruence has an impact on patients.

Social activism, especially the education of the mental health community and through them, the larger culture, about gay development can have far-reaching consequences. Charles Silverstein's impassioned argument to the nomenclature committee of the American Psychiatric Association, which did much to further the cause of deleting homosexuality as a pathological condition from that body's *Diagnostic and Statistical Manual*, is one example of this type of activism (Bayer 1981). Richard Isay's hard-fought, ten-year struggle to end discrimination against homosexuals wishing to be psychoanalysts, which was ultimately successful, is another (Isay 1994). These two instances of activism, carried out by gay dynamic psychotherapists, in combination with the work of many others, including heterosexual psychotherapists like Judd Marmor and Evelyn Hooker, have done much to lessen the psychological support that those who would continue to discriminate against homosexual people can marshal.

In short, we as psychotherapists must remember that the need for affirmation of authenticity does not end at our office doors. It is incumbent upon us to respect not only the role of amelioration, but also that of prevention. The small miracles of human acceptance that are daily achieved in our offices are of incalculable value. Ultimately, over many years, perhaps generations, these individuals who are now more accepting of themselves will change society to make it more accepting of others. However, if we simultaneously work, not only to offer our patients a relationship of acceptance and understanding, but to educate our society about the crucial importance of each person being who he or she truly is, we have the opportunity to eliminate much rejection and discrimination—and thus, spare much human suffering.

A FINAL NOTE

The work of the psychotherapist is not easy, but it is generally rewarding. The capacity of the therapist to grapple with who he or she authentically is and to accept that identity as rich, complex, and valuable, ensures both the complexity and the reward of the endeavor. This requires that we value all of our identity and experience the full range of human emotion—joy, love, and pride, as well as sadness, anger, and despair. Only through this continual life-long process of internal struggle to understand ourselves, which often necessitates our having a psychotherapist as one of the relationships in our lives, can we hope to offer a relationship to our patients that supports them in understanding themselves. Only out of our willingness to accept *our* contradictions can we offer patients the environment that will allow them to explore, and ultimately accept, theirs. Although this environment requires much to create and sustain, it also offers much in return, both to the patients who trust us with what is most precious, and often most fragile, in their lives, and ultimately to ourselves.

References

Alexander, F. (1963). *Fundamentals of Psychoanalysis*. New York: W. W. Norton.

Alexander, F., and French, T. M., with Bacon, C. L., Benedek, T., Fuerst, R. A., et al. (1974). *Psychoanalytic Therapy: Principles and Application*. Lincoln, NE: University of Nebraska Press.

Anderson, S., and Mandell, D. (1989). The use of self-disclosure by professional social workers. *Social Casework* 70:259–267.

Arlow, J. A. (1985). Some technical problems of countertransference. *Psychoanalytic Quarterly* 54:164–175.

Bayer, R. (1981). *Homosexuality and American Psychiatry: The Politics of Diagnosis*. New York: Basic Books.

Bettelheim, B. (1982). *Freud and Man's Soul*. New York: Vintage.

Blanck, G., and Blanck, R. (1974). *Ego Psychology: Theory and Practice*. New York: Columbia University Press.

Brenner, C. (1985). Countertransference as compromise formation. *Psychoanalytic Quarterly* 54:155–163.

Breuer, J., and Freud, S. (1895). Studies on hysteria. *Standard Edition* 2:1–310.

Burke, W., and Tansey, M. (1991). Countertransference disclosure and models of therapeutic action. *Contemporary Psychoanalysis* 27:351–384.

Cabaj, R. (1988). Homosexuality and neurosis: considerations for psychotherapy. *Journal of Homosexuality* 15:13–23.

Casement, P. J. (1991). *Learning from the Patient.* New York: Guilford.

Castelnuovo-Tedesco, P. (1989). The fear of change and its consequences in analysis and psychotherapy. *Psychoanalytic Inquiry* 9:101–118.

Chernus, L. (1992). The "corrective emotional experience" revisited: response of an "orthodox" self psychologist. *Clinical Social Work Journal* 20:225–228.

Chesner, S., and Baumeister, R. (1985). Effect of therapist disclosure of religious beliefs on the intimacy of client self-disclosure. *Journal of Social and Clinical Psychology* 3:97–105.

Cornett, C. (1990). The "risky" intervention: twinship selfobject impasses and therapist self-disclosure in psychodynamic psychotherapy. *Clinical Social Work Journal* 19:49–61.

——— (1992a). Orthodoxy and heresy in self psychology: a heretic's perspective. *Clinical Social Work Journal* 20:219–224.

——— (1992b). Beyond words: a conception of self psychology. *Clinical Social Work Journal* 20:337–341.

——— (1993a). Dynamic psychotherapy of gay men: a

view from self psychology. In *Affirmative Dynamic Psychotherapy with Gay Men*, ed. C. Cornett, pp. 45–76. Northvale, NJ: Jason Aronson.

_____ (1993b). "Resistance" in dynamic psychotherapy with gay men. In *Affirmative Dynamic Psychotherapy with Gay Men*, ed. C. Cornett, pp. 93–115. Northvale, NJ: Jason Aronson.

_____ (1993c). Psychotherapy of the multi-symptom patient: an integrated object relations/self psychology model. *Journal of Analytic Social Work* 1:25–37.

Cornett, C., and Hudson, R. (1987). Middle adulthood and the theories of Erikson, Gould, and Vaillant: Where does the gay man fit? *Journal of Gerontological Social Work* 10:61–73.

Cozby, P. (1973). Self-disclosure: a literature review. *Psychological Bulletin* 79:73–91.

Elson, M., ed. (1987). *The Kohut Seminars on Self Psychology and Psychotherapy with Adolescents and Young Adults*. New York: W. W. Norton.

Erikson, E. H. (1963). *Childhood and Society*, 2nd ed. New York: W. W. Norton.

_____ (1982). *The Life Cycle Completed: A Review*. New York: W. W. Norton.

Fine, R. (1982). *The Healing of the Mind: The Technique of Psychoanalytic Psychotherapy*, 2nd ed. New York: Free Press.

Frederickson, J. (1990). Hate in the countertransference as an empathic position. *Contemporary Psychoanalysis* 26:479–496.

Freud, A. (1954). Problems of technique in adult analysis. *Bulletin of the Philadelphia Association for Psychoanalysis* 4:44–70.

_____ (1966). *The Ego and the Mechanisms of Defense,* rev. ed. New York: International Universities Press.

Freud, S. (1905). Fragment of an analysis of a case of hysteria. *Standard Edition* 7:7–122.

_____ (1910). Observations on wild psychoanalysis. *Standard Edition* 11:219–227.

_____ (1912a). The dynamics of transference. *Standard Edition* 12:99–108.

_____ (1912b). Recommendations to physicians practicing psychoanalysis. *Standard Edition* 12:111–120.

_____ (1913). On beginning the treatment. *Standard Edition* 12:123–144.

_____ (1937). Analysis terminable and interminable. *Standard Edition* 23:211–253.

_____ (1940). An outline of psychoanalysis. *Standard Edition* 23:139–207.

Fricke, A. (1981). *Reflections of a Rock Lobster.* Boston: Alyson.

Friedman, R. C. (1988). *Male Homosexuality: A Contemporary Psychoanalytic Perspective.* New Haven, CT: Yale University Press.

_____ (1990). Book review of *The Psychoanalytic Theory of Male Homosexuality* by Kenneth Lewes. *Archives of Sexual Behavior* 19:293–301.

Fromm, E. (1956). *The Art of Loving.* New York: Harper and Row.

_____ (1969). *Escape From Freedom.* New York: Avon.

_____ (1976). *To Have or to Be?* New York: Bantam Books.

_____ (1980). *Greatness and Limitations of Freud's Thought.* New York: Mentor.

_____ (1989). *The Art of Being*. New York: Continuum.

Gabbard, G. O. (1990). *Psychodynamic Psychiatry in Clinical Practice*. Washington, DC: American Psychiatric Press.

Gay, P. (1988). *Freud: A Life for Our Time*. New York: W. W. Norton.

Gay, V. P. (1989). Philosophy, psychoanalysis and the problem of change. *Psychoanalytic Inquiry* 9:26–44.

Gill, M. M. (1982). *Analysis of Transference: Theory and Technique,* vol. 1. New York: International Universities Press.

Giovacchini, P. L. (1987). *A Narrative Textbook of Psychoanalysis*. Northvale, NJ: Jason Aronson.

Glover, E. (1937). Contribution to the symposium on the theory of therapeutic results of psychoanalysis. *International Journal of Psycho-Analysis* 18:125–132.

Goldberg, A. (1987). The place of apology in psychoanalysis and psychotherapy. *International Review of Psycho-Analysis* 14:409–417.

Gottesfeld, M. L. (1984). The self-psychology of Heinz Kohut: an existential reading. *Clinical Social Work Journal* 12:283–287.

Green, R. (1987). *The "Sissy Boy Syndrome" and the Development of Homosexuality*. New Haven, CT: Yale University Press.

Greenson, R. R. (1967). *The Technique and Practice of Psychoanalysis,* vol. 1. New York: International Universities Press.

Hartmann, H. (1939). *Ego Psychology and the Problem of Adaptation*. New York: International Universities Press.

Hill, C., Helms, J., Tichenor, V., et al. (1988). Effects

of therapist response modes in brief psychotherapy. *Journal of Counseling Psychology* 35:222–233.

Hoffer, A. (1985). Toward a definition of neutrality. *Journal of the American Psychoanalytic Association* 33:771–795.

Hudson, R., and Cornett, C. (1993). The process of dynamic psychotherapy with gay men living with HIV. In *Affirmative Dynamic Psychotherapy with Gay Men*, ed. C. Cornett, pp. 151–176. Northvale, NJ: Jason Aronson.

Hunter, V. (1994). Interview with Arnold Goldberg. In *Psychoanalysts Talk*, ed. V. Hunter, pp. 221–257. New York: Guilford.

Isay, R. A. (1989). *Being Homosexual: Gay Men and Their Development*. New York: Farrar, Straus, Giroux.

——— (1993a). On the analytic therapy of homosexual men. In *Affirmative Dynamic Psychotherapy with Gay Men*, ed. C. Cornett, pp. 23–44. Northvale, NJ: Jason Aronson.

——— (1993b). The homosexual analyst: clinical considerations. In *Affirmative Dynamic Psychotherapy with Gay Men*, ed. C. Cornett, pp. 177–198. Northvale, NJ: Jason Aronson.

——— (1994). *Anti-gay discrimination and organized psychoanalysis.* Paper presented at the Sixteenth National Lesbian and Gay Health Conference and Twelfth Annual AIDS/HIV Forum, New York City, June.

Jennings, C. (1993). *Understanding and Preventing AIDS.* Cambridge, MA: Health Alert Press.

Kernberg, O. F. (1975). *Borderline Conditions and Pathological Narcissism*. New York: Jason Aronson.

_____ (1980). Some implications of object relations theory for psychoanalytic technique. In *Psychoanalytic Explorations of Technique*, ed. H. Blum, pp. 207–239. New York: International Universities Press.

Kernberg, O. F., Selzer, M. A., Koenigsberg, H. W., et al. (1989). *Psychodynamic Psychotherapy of Borderline Patients*. New York: Basic Books.

Khan, M. M. (1986). Introduction. In *Holding and Interpretation: Fragment of an Analysis*, D. W. Winnicott, pp. 1–18. New York: Grove.

Kimmel, D. C. (1978). Adult development and aging: a gay perspective. *Journal of Social Issues* 34:113–130.

Kohut, H. (1971). *The Analysis of the Self*. New York: International Universities Press.

_____ (1977). *The Restoration of the Self*. New York: International Universities Press.

_____ (1984). *How Does Analysis Cure?* ed. A. Goldberg, and P. Stepansky. Chicago: University of Chicago Press.

Kubie, L. S. (1975). *Practical and Theoretical Aspects of Psychoanalysis*, rev. ed. New York: International Universities Press.

Laing, R. D. (1967). *The Politics of Experience*. New York: Pantheon.

_____ (1969). *Self and Others*. New York: Pantheon.

_____ (1971). *The Politics of the Family and Other Essays*. New York: Vintage.

Langs, R. J. (1973). *The Technique of Psychoanalytic Psychotherapy*, vol. 1. New York: Jason Aronson.

_____ (1976). *The Bipersonal Field*. New York: Jason Aronson.

_____ (1982). *Psychotherapy: A Basic Text*. New York: Jason Aronson.

Langs, R. J., and Stone, L. (1980). *The Therapeutic Experience and its Setting: A Clinical Dialogue.* New York: Jason Aronson.

Lasch, C. (1979). *The Culture of Narcissism: American Life in an Age of Diminishing Expectations.* New York: W. W. Norton.

Lieberman, E. J. (1985). *Acts of Will: The Life and Work of Otto Rank.* New York: Free Press.

Little, M. I. (1990). *Psychotic Anxieties and Containment: A Personal Record of an Analysis with Winnicott.* Northvale, NJ: Jason Aronson.

Lomas, P. (1993). *Cultivating Intuition: an Introduction to Psychotherapy.* Northvale, NJ: Jason Aronson.

―――― (1994). Psychotherapy of everyday life. *Society* 31:48–51.

Luborsky, L. (1984). *Principles of Psychoanalytic Psychotherapy: A Manual for Supportive-Expressive Treatment.* New York: Basic Books.

Malyon, A. K. (1993). Psychotherapeutic implications of internalized homophobia in gay men. In *Affirmative Dynamic Psychotherapy with Gay Men*, ed. C. Cornett, pp. 77–92. Northvale, NJ: Jason Aronson.

Masson, J. M. (1990). *Final Analysis: The Making and Unmaking of a Psychoanalyst.* Reading, MA: Addison-Wesley.

Masterson, J. F. (1976). *Psychotherapy of the Borderline Adult: A Developmental Approach.* New York: Brunner/Mazel.

Masterson, J. F., and Klein, R., eds. (1989). *Psychotherapy of the Disorders of the Self: The Masterson Approach.* New York: Brunner/Mazel.

May, R. (1953). *Man's Search for Himself.* New York: W. W. Norton.

_____ (1983). *The Discovery of Being: Writings in Existential Psychology.* New York: W. W. Norton.

McWhirter, D. P., and Mattison, A. M. (1984). *The Male Couple: How Relationships Develop.* Englewood Cliffs, NJ: Prentice-Hall.

Meissner, W. W. (1991). *What is Effective in Psychoanalytic Therapy: the Move from Interpretation to Relation.* Northvale, NJ: Jason Aronson.

Menaker, E. (1989). *Appointment in Vienna.* New York: St. Martin's Press.

Mendelsohn, R. M. (1992). *How Can Talking Help? An Introduction to the Technique of Analytic Therapy.* Northvale, NJ: Jason Aronson.

Menninger, K. A., Mayman, M., and Pruyser, P. W. (1963). *The Vital Balance: The Life Process in Mental Health and Illness.* New York: Viking.

Miller, A. (1981). *The Drama of the Gifted Child.* New York: Basic Books.

Morgan, K. S., and Nerison, R. M. (1993). Homosexuality and psychopolitics: an historical overview. *Psychotherapy* 30:133–140.

Moore, B. E., and Fine, B. D., eds. (1990a). Anonymity. In *Psychoanalytic Terms and Concepts*, p. 23. New Haven, CT: American Psychoanalytic Association and Yale University Press.

_____ (1990b). Countertransference. In *Psychoanalytic Terms and Concepts*, pp. 47–48. New Haven, CT: American Psychoanalytic Association and Yale University Press.

_____ (1990c). Impostor. In *Psychoanalytic Terms and Concepts*, p. 93. New Haven, CT: American Psychoanalytic Association and Yale University Press.

_____ (1990d). Neutrality. In *Psychoanalytic Terms and Concepts*, p. 127. New Haven, CT: American Psychoanalytic Association and Yale University Press.

_____ (1990e). Transference. In *Psychoanalytic Terms and Concepts*, pp. 196–197. New Haven, CT: American Psychoanalytic Association and Yale University Press.

_____ (1990f). True self, false self. In *Psychoanalytic Terms and Concepts*, p. 209. New Haven, CT: American Psychoanalytic Association and Yale University Press.

Nash, J. L. (1993). The heterosexual analyst and the gay man. In *Affirmative Dynamic Psychotherapy with Gay Men*, ed. C. Cornett, pp. 199–228. Northvale, NJ: Jason Aronson.

Nicolosi, J. (1993). *Healing Homosexuality: Case Stories of Reparative Therapy*. Northvale, NJ: Jason Aronson.

Ogden, T. H. (1982). *Projective Identification and Psychotherapeutic Technique*. New York: Jason Aronson.

Palombo, J. (1987). Spontaneous self-disclosures in psychotherapy. *Clinical Social Work Journal* 15:107–120.

Rako, S., and Mazer, H., eds. (1983). *Semrad: The Heart of a Therapist*. Northvale, NJ: Jason Aronson.

Ramsdell, P. S., and Ramsdell, E. R. (1993). Dual relationships: client perceptions of the effect of client–counselor relationship on the therapeutic process. *Clinical Social Work Journal* 21: 195–212.

_____ (1994). Counselor and client perceptions of the effect of social and physical contact on the therapeutic process. *Clinical Social Work Journal* 22:91–104.

Rank, O. (1964). *Will Therapy.* New York: W. W. Norton.

Reich, W. (1972). *Character Analysis,* 3rd ed., trans. V. Carfagno. New York: Simon and Schuster.

Root-Bernstein, R. D. (1993). *Rethinking AIDS: The Tragic Cost of Premature Consensus.* New York: Free Press.

Ruvelson, L. (1988). The empathic use of sarcasm: humor in psychotherapy from a self psychological perspective. *Clinical Social Work Journal* 16:297–305.

Sandler, J. (1976). Countertransference and role-responsiveness. *International Review of Psycho-Analysis* 3:43–47.

Sartre, J.-P. (1957). *Existentialism and Human Emotions.* New York: Citadel.

Schafer, R. (1983). *The Analytic Attitude.* New York: Basic Books.

Searles, H. F. (1990). The patient as therapist to his analyst. In *Classics in Psychoanalytic Technique,* rev. ed., ed. R. J. Langs, pp. 103–135. Northvale, NJ: Jason Aronson.

Silverstein, C. (1991). When the therapist is more anxious than the patient. In *Gays, Lesbians, and Their Therapists: Studies in Psychotherapy,* ed. C. Silverstein, pp. 240–252. New York: W. W. Norton.

_____ (1993). The borderline personality disorder and gay people. In *Affirmative Dynamic Psychotherapy with Gay Men,* ed. C. Cornett, pp. 117–149. Northvale, NJ: Jason Aronson.

Socarides, C. (1978). *Homosexuality.* New York: Jason Aronson.

Solomon, I. (1992a). Apology or nonapology to the patient. In *The Encyclopedia of Evolving Techniques in Dynamic Psychotherapy: The Movement to Multiple Models*, p. 21. Northvale, NJ: Jason Aronson.

—— (1992b). Neutrality. In *The Encyclopedia of Evolving Techniques in Dynamic Psychotherapy: the Movement to Multiple Models*, pp. 233–236. Northvale, NJ: Jason Aronson.

—— (1992c). Transference: general considerations. In *The Encyclopedia of Evolving Techniques in Dynamic Psychotherapy: The Movement to Multiple Models*, pp. 337–343. Northvale, NJ: Jason Aronson.

Spence, D. P. (1982). *Narrative Truth and Historical Truth: Meaning and Interpretation in Psychoanalysis*. New York: W. W. Norton.

Stanton, M. (1991). *Sandor Ferenczi: Reconsidering Active Intervention*. Northvale, NJ: Jason Aronson.

Strean, H. S., as told to Freeman, L. (1988). *Behind the Couch: Revelations of a Psychoanalyst*. New York: Wiley.

Strupp, H. H., and Binder, J. L. (1984). *Psychotherapy in a New Key: A Guide to Time-Limited Dynamic Psychotherapy*. New York: Basic Books.

Sullivan, H. S. (1953). *The Interpersonal Theory of Psychiatry*. New York: W. W. Norton.

—— (1954). *The Psychiatric Interview*. New York: W. W. Norton.

—— (1962). *Schizophrenia as a Human Process*. New York: W. W. Norton.

—— (1965). *Personal Psychopathology: Early Formulations*. New York: W. W. Norton.

Szasz, T. S. (1994a). Mental illness is still a myth. *Society* 31:34–39.

_____ (1994b). The concept of transference. In *Essential Papers on Transference Analysis*, ed. G. P. Bauer, pp. 165–194. Northvale, NJ: Jason Aronson.

Thomas, C. A., Jr., Mullis, K. B., and Johnson, P. E. (1994). What causes AIDS? It's an open question. *Reason* 26:18–23.

Van Der Leeuw, P. J. (1980). Some additional remarks on problems of transference. In *Psychoanalytic Explorations of Technique: Discourse on the Theory of Therapy*, ed. H. P. Blum, pp. 315–326. New York: International Universities Press.

Winer, R. (1994). *Close Encounters: A Relational View of the Therapeutic Process*. Northvale, NJ: Jason Aronson.

Winnicott, D. W. (1965). *The Maturational Processes and the Facilitating Environment*. New York: International Universities Press.

Wolf, E. (1988). *Treating the Self: Elements of Clinical Self Psychology*. New York: Guilford.

Yalom, I. D. (1980). *Existential Psychotherapy*. New York: Basic Books.

Index